NOTES FROM ANOTHER COUNTRY

JULIAN SYMONS

LONDON MAGAZINE EDITIONS

First published in Great Britain 1972
by London Magazine Editions
30 Thurloe Place, S.W.7
© *Julian Symons*
SBN 900626 76 3

NOTE

A Glimpse of Thirties Sunlight appeared, in a slightly different form, in *The Times Literary Supplement*. All of the other pieces were printed in the *London Magzine*. Minimal changes have been made in them, mostly to avoid repetition.

Printed in Great Britain
by Billing & Sons Limited, Guildford and London

FOR ALAN ROSS

Contents

Bonzo

In thinking of the past I am always troubled by the question: did it actually happen? Perhaps that is the wrong way to put it, for I am not in doubt about the actuality of the past but simply of my own place in it. "Some men kiss and do not tell", Lady Gregory wrote of George Moore. "George Moore does not kiss, but he tells." My trouble is rather the opposite. I find it easier to subtract from than add to the past, and what I subtract is myself. The whole thing moves before me like a film where the other actors play their parts clearly and intelligibly enough, but what should be the central figure stays indeterminate. It seems to me that I have been a watcher, not a participant, in almost all of the events that other people think of as "my" life. I feel this even about things that happened in youth, when reactions are direct and detachment is rare. I feel it about Bonzo.

I met Bonzo on Clapham Common. Forty years ago

9

the Common was a place of legend. Music hall comics used to tell jokes about it: "Have you heard the one about the nine-year-old boy who started to walk across Clapham Common one dark night and came out the other side a married man with three children?" Like many legends these had a basis of truth. Along the path that led from the top of Cedars Road, where I lived, to the fountain, and from the fountain to the bandstand, the prostitutes lined up on summer nights, those nearest the street lights young and attractive, the ones in semi-darkness visible only as shapes and creaky voices. As boys we used to tell each other about the toothless diseased creatures who hunted in the dark: "Do you know why she wears a veil, she's got no nose . . . charged him half a crown and when he asked why it was so cheap she said 'I've got me old age pension'." About the places where we played when young there is always something magical and for years the Common and the roads that led off it, roads filled with respectable red or mud-coloured Edwardian houses, was the centre of my life. Taybridge, Jedburgh, Tregarvon, Forthbridge, Stormont, Marney, the names of these roads facing the North Side of the Common sounded in my ears then like bells. Collecting friends in Taybridge or Stormont, walking up the road with them and crossing on to the Common, I had the sense of a world infinite in promise and excitement that is experienced only in youth. Here as a child, with friends named Weasel and Dicky, I crawled through the fence on to what we called the Bombing Field which had been used as a firing range in the 1914 War, and picked up old cartridge cases and puttees. Here later on I brought my first girls, furtive and acquiescent, and ploughed them into the grass. Here I played cricket on bumpy practice pitches which were supposed to cost two shillings for an evening. We played on them for nothing, keeping a lookout, and running at the approach of vengeful keepers. Here at the age of fourteen I met Bonzo.

It was an evening when as on other evenings I went out after tea, called on friends, collected cricket gear, took it on to the Common and then sat and talked until enough people had turned up to make a game. Then we picked up sides and began to play. The game was what might be called informal, with people drifting in and out of it at will and even packing up and going home if they thought they had been given out unjustly, and there were always one or two strangers who happened to be around when we picked up teams. I found myself facing one of these unknowns when I went in to bat, a fair-haired tubby figure who trotted up and projected into the air a slow high ball, well off the wicket, made for hitting. I flailed gigantically at it, missed, and the ball spun away. I watched the next ball carefully and jabbed forward, leaving a great gap between bat and pads. Through this gap the ball trickled gently, and just as gently pushed over my off stump. The bowler cupped a hand round his mouth and began to laugh, a strange sound, "Haw haw haw", that really did resemble a donkey's bray. Somebody said "Good old Bonzo", somebody else imitated his laugh. As we went on playing and he bamboozled another half dozen of us out in a similar way with slow leg breaks that spun prodigiously, I realised that Bonzo was at once respected for his bowl-

II

ing and was a kind of butt. This was particularly evident when it was his turn to bat. "Look out, here comes Hobbs", Weasel said. Bonzo patted the pitch and took guard as though he were playing in a county match instead of a knockabout. I do not remember his innings but no doubt it resembled a number of others that I saw him play, a number of elegant strokes which missed the ball, one or two that connected, a rapid retreat from any moderately fast ball pitched on his body which brought from him a cry of "Play the game, you chaps, take it easy", and ignominious dismissal when he retreated from a straight ball.

He lived in the road next to mine, and we walked home together. At first I had a disagreeable impression of him, partly because I felt that a grown man (I later learned that he was twenty-five) should not be playing with boys like us, partly because of something clownish about his appearance and behaviour. He was not really fat but his body was plump in places, rather as though he were a balloon not fully blown up. He had a large white slab of face in which all the features were indecisive, so that his blob nose and long chin might have been made out of putty. When we were alone, however, the clownishness vanished, the slab face took on a serious parsonical look and his voice too became not so much clerical as mock-clerical.

"I understand you're going to be a writer, Gus." (At this time I was always known by this farcical abbreviation of my Christian name Gustave.) "That's a fine thing to be. I am extremely interested in literature myself, I have often thought of trying a novel, although in fact

I am *more* interested still in the graphic arts." I asked uncertainly if he meant painting. "Drawings too, sketches, but I prefer to paint. In oils. More permanent. Unfortinately I may have to drop it." There was a pause before I asked why. "Next week—I tell you, Gus, but don't blab this around, you know what those silly fellows like Weasel are—I'm going up to the Oval. For a trial." He put his slab head on one side and said with a coyness that I later came to know as characteristic, "You know, Surrey have been trying for years to find a leg spinner."

The house he lived in was grey brick and we stood outside the gate talking for half an hour, opening and closing it with a slight squeak. I noticed that his clothes were shabby, not in an artistic way but distinctly down at heel, the trousers frayed and the sweater he wore patched and darned. "Forgive me for not asking you in, but I live here with Aunt Emmy, and she's not very fit," he said with his curious mock-clerical politeness. Suddenly a window was thrown up and a voice screamed: "If you're coming in you'd better come now, I'm locking up the house." I was astonished. Surely Bonzo, a grown man, would not put up with this sort of treatment. But he just made a face, lifted his shoulders as though to say that there was no accounting for the whims of sick aunts, said earnestly, "We've had a really good talk, Gus, I've enjoyed it believe me", and was gone.

During the next weeks I saw a good deal of Bonzo, and learned something about him from Weasel and Dicky. Weasel, a sharp-nosed swaggering small handsome boy who was obviously destined to be opening batsman in the cricket team we talked about forming, warned me.

"You want to watch out for him, never does a bloody stroke of work, goes down every Wednesday morning to sign on for the dole, then spends his time playing on the Common with the kids. And money—if you lend him half a dollar you'll never see it again, I tell you that." And get a trial for Surrey—Bonzo? Weasel, who surprisingly knew all about this, laughed at the idea and repeated what his bookmaker father had told him, that Bonzo was just a layabout. Dicky, who was the son of an electrician and at this time my closest friend, was more charitable. Like me, he considered himself an intellectual, and was prepared to admit Bonzo to similar status. Was he really writing a novel? Well, it was possible, and he certainly knew a lot about the writers we both read at this time, Sapper, Edgar Wallace, Dumas, Anthony Hope, Stanley J. Weyman. The Surrey trial? Dicky rubbed his big nose. "He borrowed two bob off me the other day for his fare up to the Oval, I know that." A few days later Bonzo borrowed half a crown from me. He led up to it circuitously with a long talk about Sapper ("You can't call him an artist, I should never say that, but he's a wonderful story teller") and vague references to an allowance that he would be receiving very soon, something to do with a mysterious inheritance which paid him money every quarter. Then he put his head on one side, smiled whimsically. "I say, Gus, you don't happen to be flush, do you? If you've got ten bob to spare—just till my allowance comes through. . . ." It was ridiculous, strongly reminiscent of Billy Bunter even down to the mention of an allowance, and I gave him the half crown (ten shillings would have been a fortune to me) knowing I should never see it again.

About this I was wrong. A few days later my mother called me and said: "There's a man to see you. He says he's a friend of yours", in a tone which showed distinct doubt. My mother did not approve of me having friends much older than myself and must have wondered what he was doing there anyway, calling for me at a time when respectable young men were at work. A gleaming, almost a resplendent Bonzo waited at the door—he had not been asked in. The frayed trousers and patched sweater had been replaced by a brand new brownish-mauve suit, accompanied by a gay shirt and tie and shining shoes. He plunged a hand in his pocket and pulled out an equally shining half crown. "You thought I'd forgotten, I'll bet." He put his chin in his hand and gave his "Haw haw haw", then said gravely "I always pay my debts when my ship comes home. Now let's pick up Weasel and Dicky, I've got a little surprise for you, we're going up West." And up West we went, sat in the most expensive seats at a cinema, ate an enormous meal in Lyons, rode all the way back to Clapham in a taxi. Bonzo paid for everything, and bought boxes of chocolates for us to give to our mothers, My mother was far from delighted. She looked at the chocolates suspiciously, picked one out, stared at it, bit, commented: "Soft." She liked hard centres. "Who is he then, this man, where does he get his money from, what does he do?" I evaded the questions as much as possible, knowing it would never do to say that Bonzo was on the dole and had just spent part of his quarterly allowance. Quite a large part, as it turned out. The spending period, during which he was maddeningly ebullient and assertive, buying ice creams even for those who did not want them and taking half a dozen boys out every night for sausage and chip suppers, lasted only a few days. Then he disappeared completely for a couple of weeks before sidling up to us one evening on the Common and saying, with his smile that was at once confiding and uneasy, "Hallo, you fellows." I was rather relieved somehow. It did not seem right that he should have money.

In the meantime, what about Surrey? One wet evening I was admitted to the small dark rooms in the basement of Aunt Emmy's house which he occupied. One of these was his bedroom and in the other he lived and occasionally cooked food on a spirit stove. This living-room contained a curious collection of books, mostly thrillers but including Edward Bellamy and William Morris, several books on theosophy, and Morley's life of Gladstone which he told me was a work of genius, the greatest biography ever written. In one corner what was said to be one of his oil paintings, a country scene with cows, stood on an easel. Brushes lay beside it, but I never saw Bonzo put brush to canvas, and I later believed that he picked up the painting in a junk shop. Admittance to these rooms was an unusual favour, for Aunt Emmy was frantically irritated by the presence of strangers down below and would make her displeasure felt by shrieking orders down the stairs: "I want those potatoes *now*, not next week", or "If you want any supper you can go and do the shopping." At these words Bonzo would rise from an old broken-springed sofa on which he often lay and talked about life, art and cricket, call up some placating words, and say with an air of resignation and in his mock-clerical tone, "Awfully sorry, my dear fellow, but you know the old girl's not very fit, mustn't upset her." On this evening, however, Aunt Emmy was silent. Bonzo had brewed some tea and was talking about the perfect grace of Frank Woolley, and of Weasel's likeness to him as a batsman, when I broke in to ask rather brutally: what about Surrey? Bonzo smiled his smile, wriggled on the sofa, spoke,

"Saturday week. The Essex match."

Did I believe him? Certainly I wished to believe and as he told me the tale of success in his last trial game, of bowling Alan Peach twice in half a dozen balls and of Andy Sandham's inability to pick out his wrong 'un, belief grew. In the end I asked the question I was longing to have answered. "Did you bowl to Hobbs?"

Bonzo at once became preternaturally grave, lowering his voice as though we were in church. He shook his head slowly. "He wasn't in the nets. I don't think I should fancy bowling to Jack Hobbs. Saturday week then, and shall I tell you something, Gus? I shan't mind if we lose the toss, I want a spinner's wicket." He flexed his fingers. I saw the Essex wickets tumbling.

A week passed, but where was Bonzo? Not on the Common, not at home when I rapped on his basement door. At the Oval perhaps, turning his arm over a few more times in preparation for Saturday, baffling Sandham time and again with his wrong 'un. On Friday night the Surrey team was announced in the paper. His name was not mentioned, not even as twelfth man. I had known it all the time of course, in a way, but still my disappointment was intense. A few days latter he re-appeared on the Common, smiling his uneasy smile, and performing a little trick he had of making the ball run down his arm, over his shoulders and down the other arm. I did not speak to him, but somebody else did. "Hey, Bonzo, what's happened, thought you were play-ing for Surrey."

Bonzo's doughy features were screwed up in a look of astonishment and martyrdom. "Didn't you fellows hear?"

"What?"

"They picked Gregory instead. Can't have two leg spinners." And in fact R. J. Gregory did begin a long, successful career for Surrey in this match, first as a leg break bowler and later as a most competent batsman. Later on I often wondered whether there had been any-thing in Bonzo's story. Did he at least have a trial and bamboozle Sandham just once with a googly? It is not likely, because Bonzo's expression when attempting a googly was one of agonised concentration combined with obvious guile, but I like to think it may have been so.

After that we heard no more of Surrey, but our cricket team became a reality and we let Bonzo play for it, although he was so much older than the rest of us. There was some opposition, chiefly on the ground that it was unfair to our opponents, none of whom was more than eighteen, but what finally settled it was the great usefulness of Bonzo. He made himself responsible for most of the gear, sometimes staggering under the weight of a heavy bag for a mile or more. He blancoed pads, mended bats, repaired gloves, was always first at the meeting place for away matches, slab faced and smiling.

18

He was also much our most successful bowler, mesmerising most of the teams we played against with his huge leg breaks. The voice most often raised against him was that of Weasel, our best batsman. Indeed, it was noticeable that the more Bonzo praised Weasel's batting ability the ruder Weasel was to Bonzo. One day when Bonzo was not there and half a dozen of us lay on the Common watching the passing girls and speculating which of them would do it and which wouldn't, Weasel said: "You know what he is, Bonzo, don't you? He's a nance."

A nancy boy! I could not believe it. The only nancy boy I knew of was a man named Orlando Merrill, who lived in Taybridge Road, was said to be an actor, and walked in a fastidious mincing manner. When Orlando passed by, Weasel and one or two others would always go after him, holding their clothes tightly to their bodies and asking falsetto: "How do I look? Fancy me tonight, dear?" Bonzo was not in the least like this, and I said so. Weasel laughed. "Course he's a nance. What d'you think he's always hanging round us for? You ought to hear what some of my dad's friends say about him."

"What does your dad let you go about with him for, then?" Dicky asked.

"I can look after myself, mate." And nobody looking at Weasel's little handsome face, the features classically fixed as though made from cast iron, could have doubted it.

When Bonzo turned up again I looked at him with Weasel's words in mind, but he was still the same Bonzo, good-tempered and obliging, sometimes quite maddening with his secret smiles and his "Haw haw haw", a bit of a fake perhaps, but surely harmless. One day I

19

showed him some poems I had written. He took them away to read, and later became super-parsonical.

"I like some of these, I like them very much indeed. It s a wonderful thing to be a poet. Do you know what Shelley called them? 'The unacknowledged legislators of mankind'."

"Did he?" The phrase meant nothing to me.

"Sapper is a fine writer, and so is Jeffery Farnol, but Shelley was better. And Rupert Brooke too, you ought to read his stuff. Have you read him? Or Tennyson?"

"A bit."

"Here." He produced a volume bound in limp red leather, pushed it at me and walked away. It was Tennyson's *Idylls of the King*. Inside he had written: "Gus the poet, from his friend Bonzo."

I should like to be able to say that I was touched by this gift, but the truth is that it increased my doubts about Bonzo, and that I never thanked him properly for it, only saying nastily that I didn't think much of Tennyson. When his next allowance came along I rejected an offer to go up West, and so only heard about the great spending splurge lasting four days in which he took boys to theatres and cinemas and to the Zoo, and ended up by buying Weasel, who had been on every one of the expeditions, an air gun. When the money had gone he came shambling up to the Common again, smiling and saying he was temporarily hard up and would like to borrow half a crown.

What more is there to say about Bonzo? A great deal, I am sure, for conversations with him filled my life that summer, but somehow the heart of our relationship evades me. I don't know at all what I felt for him, any more than I know where his allowance came from or whether he was really a homosexual. I remember the shock I had one day when I found him serving behind the counter at our grocer's shop, looking very clean and spruce and attending to customers with lavish over-politeness, but this job, like others which he held, lasted only a couple of weeks. What stays with me most clearly is a purely visual recollection of long evenings on the Common, a silent picture in colour, the sky melting into a mess of red and gold, twilight changing to darkness, trams running like golden beetles along North Side to the Plough. I remember away games, Bonzo turning up without money for his fare and staggering under the weight of cricket bags, saying half-seriously: "Come on you fellows, give a hand, my spinning finger's paralysed." And of course I remember him bowling, the would-be fierce expression on the doughy face when he was hit to the boundary, the chin cupped in hand when he had puzzled or beaten the batsman, the ball flipped from toe to hand or rolled down his back after he had taken a wicket. All this belongs to the surface, and it is only the surface of a relationship that I can offer. Let me move on to the trivial, shameful end.

The last match of the season was played away, and we won. Bonzo took several wickets and Weasel made quite a lot of runs. "Haw haw haw" sounded rather often, and as always success made Bonzo irritatingly inclined to go over the details of the game, bathing every boundary and wicket in the golden light of retrospect. "Did you see the look on that geezer's face when I got him leg before with my top spinner? And that chap with the doodahs on his cap, wasn't he surprised when I bowled him round his legs?" Two or three of us told him to shut up, but he continued to replay the match until we got back to Clapham. Then, walking down the long road that cuts across the Common he began to extol Weasel's innings. "The way you turned that fast bowler off your legs, it was just beautiful."

"Shut your trap", Weasel said.

"Now then. Little boys shouldn't talk like that to their elders and betters." Bonzo made a grab for Weasel, as he often did, pulled him on to the grass and began to wrestle with him playfully. Weasel got up and kicked him. His face was red.

"Ow." Bonzo really did say "Ow" as he got up rubbing his leg where he had been kicked. "What's got into you?"

"You just fucking well keep away from me, that's all."

"Little boys shouldn't swear," Bonzo said with his maddening coyness. He never swore himself.

"You know what you are, you're a bloody layabout. That's what my dad says." Bonzo shook his head with an injured ironical smile suggesting that dads might say anything, there was no accounting for dads. Weasel picked up a stone. "So fuck off." He threw the stone. It hit Bonzo on the thigh. He yelped like a dog and retreated.

"Good shot," somebody said. There was a murmur of laughter. Weasel picked up a handful of stones and a couple of friends of his picked some up too. They began to throw them, Weasel with vigour, his friends halfheartedly. Bonzo was not hit, but he moved behind some bushes.

Hopping from one leg to another and dodging around the bushes he said "Hold on, you fellows", and "Pack it in now, a joke's a joke", and "I shall have to teach you a lesson, young Weasel, I can see that."

"I'll teach you a bloody lesson." Weasel was furious. More boys picked up stones, there was a regular small fusillade. Bonzo's antics looked extremely comic, and nobody except Weasel threw with the idea of hitting him. I think several of us felt that there was something undignified and wrong about Bonzo's behaviour, that just as he ought really to have played cricket with those of his own age, so he should now have fired back at us more powerful and damaging stones than those we threw at him. I did not throw a stone myself, but stood and watched. Bonzo suddenly gave a cry, clapped a hand to his cheek and dropped down behind the bushes.

The stone throwing stopped. There was silence. One of Weasel's friends said, "You hit him, Weasel, you threw it." Weasel muttered something. We approached. As we got near Bonzo lifted his head fearfully. A stone must have nicked his cheek, which had a slight smear of blood on it, but that was not why we stared. Bonzo was crying. Tears rolled from his eyes. His shoulders shook with sobs.

"A bloody cry baby," Weasel said. "Come on, let's go home."

We moved away across the Common and left him. I turned round once and saw him get up, wipe his eyes and shamble away. He never played with us again.

After I left Clapham I did not see Bonzo for years. Then one evening as I reached the bottom of the escalator at Leicester Square Underground I heard a cry: "Gus, hey there, Gus." I looked round and there, a comic revenant masquerading in a London Transport uniform, was Bonzo. He had grown immensely fat, the old coy smile was there but buried in layers of blubber, one button was off his uniform and as in the old days his trousers were frayed.

"And how's the world been treating you, Gus, can't call you Julian. Pretty well, from all I hear." The old "Haw haw haw" sounded more raucous than it had in my youth. How long had he been working for London Transport? Years and years, he would soon be in line for a pension. When I said that he had found a permanent job at last his features took on the injured expression I remembered, but it was soon replaced by his confiding look. He put a hand on my arm.

"Tell you something else. You knew I was married?"

"No."

"You must meet the wife, we often talk about you. But what I wanted to say was this. I've got three boys and Joe—he's the eldest, seventeen—is quite exceptional. I want to do something for him if I can, use my influence." I moved uneasily. What did Joe want, a job in publishing? I should have known better. "Quite seriously, Gus," the mock-clerical voice said, "Quite seriously, and I'm not exaggerating, Joe's the best leg break bowler in the country."

A Death

My parents quarrel in the neighbour room. Whenever I read that line of Stephen Spender's it brings to my mind an evening when I was nearly sixteen and heard my mother and father talking about me. I must have been in the living-room of our gloomy large Clapham house while they were in the kitchen next to it, although I cannot remember the place but only the voices. *Whatever shall we do,* my mother said and repeated, *What shall we so with him, how will he ever get a job?* My father answered in his throaty guttural tone, and he must have said something consolatory because it was not in his nature to be anything but cheerful, but she asked again how I would ever get a job and said that somebody should do something for me, help me to become a journalist. But then it was obvious that I should never become a journalist, I should never get a job. Defeated, my father raised his voice, which was his usual response to any inconvenient statement. She began to weep and then I suppose I went out of the living-room. I hated, then as now, to hear people emotionally close to me quarrelling.

When would I ever get a job? The problem was not my stupidity but my stammer. At the age of three I had been able to repeat and recite little stretches of verse, but two years later this parlour achievement had disappeared, leaving behind it a stammer which made it difficult for me to speak a couple of consecutive sentences. Stammer is not quite the right word, for what afflicted me was a hesitation that often made it impossible for me to say anything at all. My mother had no doubt that the trouble had its origin in my being, as she said, brought on too fast. When it persisted she took me to a doctor who advised speech therapy which involved singing words instead of speaking them, and when this failed, to a specialist who recommended the use of a curiously shaped device resembling a bent glass ruler. With this held over my tongue I spoke semi-audibly a variety of words chosen for their consonantal difficulty—"s" and "g" at the beginning of words were my worst problems. After this device proved ineffective she gave up trying to cure the hesitation by physical means, and for the most part it was ignored. My father could never quite believe that the whole thing was not deliberate, and would sometimes burst out into angry shouting ("Come on, sir, say what you've got to say, get it out"), but generally the trouble was left to cure itself. The discussion on this particular evening was caused by the fact that I had emerged from a commercial school as an efficient shorthand typist, but had been turned down for half a dozen jobs because I was unable to answer questions. Obviously I should never become a journalist and I don't think I particularly wanted to be one, although I said that I did.

What is the origin of a stammer, if one accepts the word as covering my inability to speak? "Excitement, fear, or constitutional defect", says the Shorter Oxford, but I have come to think of it as the expression of some deep dissociation of sensibility, based perhaps in my own case on the fact that as a baby I was put out to nurse for some months because there were too many children about the house for my mother to look after, perhaps on my situation as much the youngest of my family, an unwanted although not after my arrival unloved child. And it may be that the best thing to do about such a stammer is to ignore it. Certainly the specific worked, more or less, in my case. A year or so before this time I began to go around with girls, and I generally managed not to stammer in their presence. Slowly, slowly, the hesitation faded in other company. Today I hesitate when upset or excited, I still find it difficult to say *Goodbye* on the telephone, and I approach an appearance on radio or television with pure terror, but for the most part I can talk fluently enough, although in what seems to me when I hear it recorded, a very curious voice. There are many people who have never heard me stammer, and find it hard to believe that I ever did. Shortly after that kitchen conversation which I overheard I applied for another job, survived the interview without a trace of hesitation in speech, and was engaged as a shorthand typist at twenty-seven and sixpence a week.

The firm at which I went to work was housed in

Spenser Street, a mews at the back of Victoria Street. On the ground floor a number of secondhand dynamos and bits of electric motors were littered about a dirty worshop. At the side of this workshop narrow dark stairs ascended to a large office much of which was occupied by a square oak desk, a smaller office which was used as a showroom, and a cubby hole between them which had no window but was faintly illuminated by a skylight. The firm's bold, impressive writing paper said that they were electric motor and dynamo engineers, contractors to H.M. Government, and agents for Puyrelite Lighting Fittings.

All this was true but it was also a deception, for V.L.D. (Victoria Lighting and Dynamos) specialised in buying things cheap and selling them dear. The dynamos we sold were in three categories. The best, which were guaranteed for twelve months and said to be "absolutely as new", had seen a good deal of hard wear but generally survived their twelve months' guarantee period before breaking down. The second best, "really first-class machines which can be strongly recommended", were pretty much beaten up and often gave trouble during their six months guarantee period. The machines in the third category, "in very good running order" but sold without guarantee, were quite frankly on their last legs and frequently needed a complete armature rewind before they had been in service a month.

The firm was owned by Mr. Budette, a bluff Germanic Englishman in spite of his name. He was a man who had a real gift of persuasiveness, which extended to himself. When he was selling a dynamo salvaged from a building site and cursorily done up in the workshop he really did believe that he was offering a machine which was a bargain at the price he asked, and on the rare occasions when we had something to offer that was in first-class condition, a sceptical buyer would make him frantic with regret at the chance the prospective purchaser was missing. "I can't let you say no to this one, it's such a snip," he would say with perfect sincerity. "Come round to the Albert and talk about it, we've just got to do a deal." At the Albert, a handsome pub on the corner of Victoria Street and Buckingham Gate, cronies would be met, much whisky and beer would be drunk, and often a deal would be done. Returning with the client after the pub closed at three, full of booze and jollity, Mr. Budette would say: "You've driven a hard bargain, old man, but I respect you for it." Nobody was sorrier, nobody more astonished, than Mr. Budette when the dynamo developed a little trouble.

It may sound as though he should have been rich, but the business provided no more than a comfortable living, and he was always looking for ideas that would make his fortune. At various times he persuaded people to put money into several of these ideas. One of them was a small electric lavatory fan placed just below the seat, which was activated as the incumbent rose from it, another was a cure for hay fever by electrical ionisation of the nasal membranes, and a third was the sale of Puyre-lite Lighting fittings, a German product for which he held the sole British agency. At the time of my arrival the Kleenair Toilet Fan had been designed and tested and was in course of production under the financial umbrella of Miss Gregory, a small, grim-faced sharp-nosed spinster who had put several hundred pounds into K.T.F.C. (Kleenair Toilet Fan Company), a subsidiary company of V.L.D. Miss Gregory had come as book-keeper to V.L.D. but had soon invested money in K.T.F.C., convinced by Mr. Budette s confident assurance that it would be quadrupled within a few months.

But the fan which had worked perfectly in Mr. Budette's own lavatory proved much less tractable when confronted with a different type of pan, a different shape of seat. Sometimes it did not start at all, sometimes it started and refused to stop, and in many cases it failed to dissipate the fumes. As money was spent on costly experiments and the fan was redesigned to include a different switch-on and cut-out device, Miss Gregory's knife-like nose grew sharper and her nutcracker face more severe. She sat on the other side of the big oak desk from Mr. Budette (I was housed in the cubby hole with the skylight) and glared across at him with her little steel-coloured eyes. Sometimes I would hear them arguing when she reproached him for returning late from an Albert lunch, more than once I entered the room to find her in tears. Mr. Budette was distressed by this, for he was a happy man himself and liked other people to be happy too. Looking back, I think that he gave up hope of the Kleenair Fan shortly after my arrival, but he would be driven by her tears into brief bursts of energy, visits to the fan motor manufacturers, returns to the drawing board, modifications of the design that had seemed so promising, long talks with wholesalers which were conducted from his side on the assumption that the fan was a certain success instead of an unproved experiment. From these talks he returned with assurances of interest, tentative orders for the time when K.T.F.C. was in full production, which placated Miss Gregory for a few days. But the end was inevitable. The capital she had invested melted away, Mr. Budette lost interest in the whole idea and became absorbed by the possibilities of the hay-fever cure, to which he was introduced by the young doctor who had invented the ionisation technique, a psychiatrist attached to a Government prison. The Kleenair Fan project was abandoned, and some eighteen months after my arrival Miss Gregory left the firm. Her place at the other side of the oak desk was taken by a friend of the doctor, a man named York, who put up a thousand pounds so start the Pimlico Clinic for the treatment of hay fever. I became book-keeper, and later nominally company secretary, to both V.L.D. and the Pimlico Clinic. I received what seemed to me an enormous increase in my wage packet, first up to forty and then to fifty shillings a week.

Did Mr. Budette really want to make money? I don't think so. As long as he had enough to keep his family in the suburban comfort of Upper Norwood and to sustain those long sessions in the Albert, he was content. He wanted to make a fortune quickly, but that is rather different from a serious desire to make money. What beckoned him on was the prospect at the end of the journey, but it was the details of the journey itself that he enjoyed—obtaining financial backing, devising elaborate agreements providing for the division of future profits, working out sales campaigns. I doubt if he ever truly expected to arrive. Sometimes he would look round our dusty shabby offices in the hard light of early morning and say to me: "We're going to have a new régime here, Symons. I'm going to make a clean sweep." We would get rid of the worst junk in the workshop (which was always called "the works"), obtain an agency from a German firm for a cheap and marvellously efficient line in dynamos, install sparkling new machines. But in a few days he would have sold for thirty pounds an old dynamo that we had bought for three, and the new régime would be forgotten. As time went by—and I stayed at V.L.D. for what seems in retrospect an incredibly long time, eleven years—life became harder, prospects fewer, capital more difficult to obtain, but none of this quenched Mr. Budette's enthusiasm, and his certainty that fortune lay round the corner. He was one of the few genuine optimists I have known.

My father was another. It may well be that I stayed at V.L.D. so long because Mr. Budette was in many ways a father surrogate, replacing my actual parent's shouting irascibility with an invariable pig-like equability of temperament. To this day I know very little about our family origins, beyond the facts that my father was a Russian or Polish Jew, that he came to England some time in his youth and that his name was not Symons. Was it really Brann or Brand or Lander? They were all names that he used at different times. Was he a master linen-draper or a picture-frame maker? He called himself both these things in a period before I was born, and I suppose may have followed such occupations. Did he change his
32

name to Simmons or Symons when he was naturalised, was he ever naturalised at all? It is impossible to check naturalisation details at Somerset House unless you know the original name. Short, ruddy, fair, neatly bearded, thin in youth but pot-bellied in middle age (he was nearly fifty when I was born), he mastered the English language but could not easily manage its vowels, so that he always said "cutn" for cotton and "dunt" for don't. My mother was English, but I know nothing of her background beyond the fact that she had some French and some Spanish blood. Before I was born, in a time remembered by my brothers and sister, they had run secondhand clothing shops which failed, failures which necessitated sudden departures from Peckham and Ladywell and no doubt other parts of London. My mother had no relatives, my father was estranged from his. "Differences, never reconciled and never explained, cut my father off even from correspondence with the majority of his blood relations", my eldest brother, A. J., wrote long afterwards. It appeared to me that we had no relatives, and certainly we had very few friends.

It was a strange family life, but it did not seem strange to me at the time. Almost my first memories are of the secondhand clothing shop we had in Tyneham Road, Battersea (my father was now describing himself accurately enough as a "general dealer") and the small house just round the corner in Lavender Hill where we lived, and I vividly remember our removal when I was six years old to the box-like large grey house no more than half a mile away in Cedars Road, Clapham. The acquisition of this solid Victorian house represented an enormous change in our fortunes. In the 1914–18 War my father made, probably for the first time, what was by his standards a lot of money by selling secondhand clothing, then furniture, typewriters, anything he could lay hands on. He bought an auction room in Moorgate and became an auctioneer, conducting sales very successfully, he filled the Clapham house with ornate furniture, he became the owner of four racehorses. We had an Overland car and a chauffeur to drive it. In the Overland he went to the race meetings he loved, whether or not his own horses were running. On Sunday mornings local acquaintances, and men met at Moorgate who had plans for making a lot of money quickly, came to drink champagne in the drawing-room. It was a far cry from the shop in Tyneham Road but I accepted it all incuriously, as children accept anything that happens to them. I noticed nothing odd in my father's pronunciation, and did not realise that there was anything unusual about somebody in our position owning racehorses. After all, I had read the *Sporting Life* from the age of six.

From as early as I can remember I was frightened of him. Immensely genial and generous with business and racing associates he was short-tempered at home, shouting angrily about mistakes made or things left undone, savagely censorious in relation to any friend brought back to the house, prudish in a deep-seated Jewish way about sexual matters. I found no refuge except in tears from his irrational anger. If he saw me playing solitary games with soldiers on the bedroom floor he would tell me to get them cleared up and do some work, when I was reading an article about Napoleon's Marshall Lannes

34

in the *Encyclopaedia Britannica* he took the volume from me, turned the pages until he found the name of Linnaeus and, frantic with irritation, said: "Read *that*, sir, read something useful." How did he know about Linnaeus, why should he have thought knowledge of Linnaeus more useful than knowledge of Lannes? He had many odd snatches of knowledge and his conversation was spotted with quotations, or phrases that sounded like quotations ("He knows who knows that he knows nothing" he would often say when rebuking A. J.'s youthful pretensions), yet these were notable really because of the great areas of his ignorance. "Anthology, sir, what kind of word is that?" he asked when A. J. published his *Anthology of Nineties Verse*.

The family prosperity didn't last long. The horses were ruinously expensive. Within a couple of years they had gone. With them went the car, and soon afterwards the Moorgate Auction Rooms. He turned to keeping a small hotel on the front at Brighton, where I was sent, because of my speech defect, to a school for backward children, then to running a bookmaking business with my brother Maurice as partner (he refused to lay off bets on horses which he thought would lose and the business packed up within twelve months), then back to running a Soho auction room without success. Desperate for money, he sold off part of our Cedars Road garden to a local builder, mortgaged the house, gave a Bill of Sale on the contents. When payments fell due he was sometimes unable to make them, and A. J. was called into urgent consultation to provide or somehow borrow the money. Without ever going hungry we became poorer and poorer. How did we survive the 'twenties, a decade in the latter part of which he made almost no money? Partly by letting off rooms in the house partly by the money brought in by those of us who lived at home. My mother made it clear both that this money was indispensable, and at the same time that it by no means paid for our keep. My father took no part in such explanations. Like Mr. Budette he was less interested in the present than in the fortune seen mistily in the near distance, but he had no V.L.D. to fall back on when the prospect dissolved.

One day he fell over and broke his leg. It mended badly, and afterwards he always walked with a stick. A few months later he had his first heart attack, a slight one. The doctor advised a quiet life, a diet, no alcohol. My father ignored these injunctions. How could he obey them when excitement, the excitement of profit and loss, was the thing he lived for? He limped down Cedars Road every morning, took the bus up to Soho, hung round the Greek Street auction rooms (later the site of the Establishment), drank with his friends, did a little betting on horses that they told him couldn't lose, talked about ways of raising the wind, limped hime again. He had a second heart attack, and a third. They always occurred in the night, and he became nervous about going to bed.

What did he feel about his family? Probably he was disappointed in all of his sons except A. J. He throve on rows, the passionate expression of feeling, furious anger followed by expansive gestures of reconciliation and forgiveness, and only A. J. was able to shout back at him, to give as good as he got in a slanging match and to feel no aftertaste of malice or bitterness. The rest of his sons were cowed but resentful, and I was the most cowed of all. Perhaps he sounds a delightful character put down in print, and in many ways I suppose he was: but he was totally unsympathetic and unhelpful to me, and indeed the very idea that a father might be "helpful" to his sons would have seemed to him ridiculous. As much as I hated anybody at this time of my life, I hated my father.

His heart attacks brought me up against the reality of illness and possible death for the first time. When I was a child the night held terrors for me as it does for many, and they were revived by the circumstances of his heart attacks, my mother's urgent knocking on the bedroom door at two in the morning, the telephone call for the doctor, the bearded figure in the double bed gasping with pain, all colour drained away, consciousness of my own uselessness at the bedside, relief at the doctor's arrival and greater relief when, shaken and shivering, I was allowed to go back to bed. In the morning he would be sleeping, for two or three days he would stay in bed and then he would be up again and around the house, shouting at everybody. Within a week he would be limping off again to Soho in search of his lost fortune.

From this stifling enclosed life I escaped in the summer to play cricket on Clapham Common, in the winter to the Temperance Billiards Hall at the bottom of Cedars Road, where I played snooker. In the autumn and winter I spent almost every evening down there until midnight when the hall closed. Then with half a dozen other boys I went to a café nearby to eat pie and baked beans, or to look for girls on the Common. These excursions into low life, like my feeling for Mr. Budette, were I suppose a reaction to my relationship with my father, who also found himself very much at ease in vulgar company. My behaviour worried my mother, to whose questions about where I had been I returned evasive replies, but I don't know that my father was ever much interested. Perhaps, now that I was firmly fixed in a job, he had given me up.

Returning one December night in 1929 from such an evening I found him alone in the living room, reading. My mother was in bed with a violent migraine headache, and he had picked up Louis Marlow's *The Lion Took Fright*, which I had got from the public library. "Don't think much of *this*," he said dismissively. "Silly book." He lingered deliberately, as he often did in those days, but half an hour later we both went to bed. At three o'clock my mother pounded on the bedroom door. He had had another heart attack.

I put on a dressing gown and went shivering downstairs to the room where he lay. Everything was as it had been before when my brother Maurice, my sister and I stood round the chalky-faced figure in the bed. With uncharacteristic consideration he gasped, "Sorry to cause so much trouble", and went back to struggling with his pain. The doctor came, injected, went again. My sister made a cup of tea for my mother, whose migraine had vanished under the stress of the heart attack. She stayed to watch beside him, and the rest of us went back to bed. I was sound asleep when she woke me at about six o'clock. "He's

38

gone", she said, "He's gone." For a few moments I did not understand what she meant.

In the morning A. J., who was married and living away from home, came over and took charge. He made all the arrangements for the funeral and comforted my mother, who determinedly continued her Christmas preparations. "He always did what he wanted to do," A. J. said to her. "And that's the only thing that matters in life." Is it? I was impressed by the words at the time but have never been convinced of their truth nor been able to carry them through in my own life, perhaps because I have never really wanted anything enough. Mr. Budette gave me a couple of days off from work and I hung dismally about the house, paying one sneaking visit to the Billiards Hall which would greatly have upset my mother had she known of it. Following the coffin to Wandsworth Cemetery I was not conscious of deep sorrow, nor of any emotion except ignoble relief, and a feeling that life might be easier now. By one of the few provident acts of his life my father had taken out the deeds of the Cedars Road house in my mother's name. He left nothing but a few debts, which A. J. paid. His personal estate was valued at four pounds.

A Prolonged Adolescence

It is two years now since my brother Maurice died. He was next to me in age among our family, and although the difference was eight years, he took me around with him a great deal when I was a boy. It was with Maurice that I went to Stamford Bridge and shouted for Chelsea, Maurice who took me to the Oval on an August Bank Holiday to see George Gunn strolling down the pitch. Now that he is gone, I thought as I travelled on the M.1 up to Northampton to attend the funeral, nobody I know will be able to name the Chelsea team in 1921, as he and I could. This and similar absurdities touched me, conveying as they did the recollection of many kindnesses in my youth that at the time I had taken for granted, and that I had not thought about for years.

After the funeral I went through his papers. Maurice, it turned out, had been a compulsive hoarder. He was a great collector of cigarette cases and lighters, and one whole drawer was filled with cases that had evidently been put by rather than discarded. Another drawer was filled with old wallets, and others with papers and records dealing with our careers as table tennis players. I settled upon these, probing with fascination into an uncertainly remembered past. He had kept the programme of the 1934 English Open Championship, in which he had been knocked out early on by the champion Victor Barna, but (I was surprised to see) I had reached the last sixteen, losing then narrowly against an English international I had always personally disliked. Maurice was a better and more consistent player than I, but just for this one season I was really very good.

I learned to play the game on a table top in a spare room of our Clapham house, using a plain wooden bat. We played only against each other, we both hit the ball very hard, and decided that we must be among the best dozen players in England. Disillusionment came when first Maurice and then I joined a local club, and found that we could not always beat moderate club players. Within a few months however, this had changed, and inside a couple of years we had founded our own club. It was called Clapham, and it moved quickly from the second to the first division of the London League. In this division we were runners-up in the 1934 season to West Ealing, a team composed almost wholly of internationals.

Table tennis was and remains an extremely democratic game. All you need is a large room with an even floor surface, and comparatively inexpensive equipment. When I played, most of the best teams were attached to tennis clubs, like West Ealing and Herga, or were part of a social club like the East End Jewish team, the Old Victorians. Our Clapham team had its headquarters first in a local pub and then in a Temperance Billiards Hall. Table tennis was unmarked by distinctions of class or cash, although there were one or two teams who did not much relish going down to play the Old Victorians. The democratic nature of table tennis is essentially unchanged, but the game itself is very different from the one I played. It has become much faster, thanks largely to the spread of the penholder grip, which in my time was regarded almost as a curiosity. Speed has triumphed over elegance and finesse, as it has done in lawn tennis, but it has at least emphasised that success depends on aggression. This was not so in the early 'thirties. In one World Championship match a Polish player named Ehrlich, with a fine defence but sketchy attacking strokes, met a similarly equipped Rumanian named Paneth. Neither was prepared to risk a hit, and their first game took more than seven hours, with both players pushing the ball over the net. After losing this game Paneth suffered an emotional collapse, and the rest of the match was over in five minutes. As a direct consequence of the many farcical games in this championship a time-limit rule was introduced. Was it in 1934 or 1935? The *Guinness Book of Records* is silent about the longest game ever played, and there is no official history of the game. Maurice's papers also were silent upon the subject.

They documented faithfully, however, my one very good year. Playing number one for Clapham (Maurice was number two) I beat David Jones, at that time the English champion, in a League match, and narrowly lost to him in the semi-final of the London championship. I was one of the twenty-odd players picked to compete, in true democratic fashion, for places in the national team to play for the Swaythling Cup, the Davis Cup of table tennis. I had a triumphant first day, winning every match I played, and was included in the ten players from whom five were to be chosen. I had blotted out from my memory what happened at the second trials, but Maurice's papers recorded that I lost every game. He had kept also a note written to him by one of the selectors, expressing doubt that I was good enough to be chosen for the trials in the first place. I daresay the selector was right.

These trials, and my play in the English Open, were in any case the peak of my table tennis performance. The decline was sharp. In the 1935 season the *South London Press* headline: "G. J. Symons Disappoints in Tournament", might have been repeated several times. I beat nobody of any consequence, and did badly in League matches. Did I play on for one more season? I can't remember, but if so I did no better. Maurice, however, went on playing, and in his middle thirties even improved. He wrote a book on the game, became a well-known coach, and marketed the M. A. Symons table tennis bat. Like me, though, he left unfulfilled his ambition to play for England.

The thing I regret most in my life is the lack of deep and high creative talent as a writer. Next to that (incongruous follow-up!) I regret my failure to excel at any game. The summers of my youth were spent playing cricket enthusiastically but badly, the winter evenings found me playing table tennis or bent over the tables at the Lavender Hill Temperance Billiards Hall, although the game I played was snooker. I was good enough at snooker to scrape into the very strong local team two or three times, but so far as I remember I never won a game.

Temperance Billiards Halls—the one at Lavender Hill was not our table tennis headquarters—have almost disappeared. They had their origins in the Victorian temperance movement, and were part of the attempt to separate enjoyment from alcohol. South London was rich in these squat, forceful, fanciful buildings which often formed the centrepiece for a row of shops—I remember the halls in Clapham, Streatham, Battersea Rise and Brixton, all within a couple of miles of Lavender Hill—and although a pub might be nearby, the ban on alcohol was strictly observed. Some fairly tough characters used the Lavender Hill hall, but although there were occasional fights, in one or two of which I saw knives drawn, the atmosphere was essentially one of settled calm. The four tables in the outer hall were the showpieces of the place. There a gambler known as Jack the Fiddler, who impressed me by invariably wearing a silk shirt, would give anybody a handicap of one to four blacks, and play him for a fiver. His opponents would be Mac the local fishmonger, Ron the garage-owner, one or another sharp young boy who had found a couple of backers. Billiards was played very little, and more chancy games like Russian pool were viewed with contempt, although they were sometimes played on the fourteen tables of the inner room. The police paid occasional visits, but rarely did more than look around. Snooker was the
44

thing, and it was played seriously. The bets were serious enough—I generally came out winning or losing a pound, which was a lot of money to me in those days—yet even for a professional like Jack the Fiddler the game was what mattered. The expression on his broad knife-scarred face, after he had put down a red and played to get perfect position on the black, was surely one of aesthetic rather than mercenary pleasure.

The Temperance Halls closed at midnight. At the week-end, when I had the whole of my wages, I would leave with half a dozen friends a few minutes before closing time, eat a pie and beans at a local café, and then go to the house of one friend or another to play cards until six or seven in the morning. From these sessions of solo, brag or slippery sam, I would emerge sometimes with only a shilling or two left, more often (or is that an illusion?) showing a handsome profit. But if I did make money, that was not the true object of the exercise, any more than it was at snooker. Partly it was just that I liked to win, but partly also that my companions, who included a lorry driver, a milkman, and a bookmaker's clerk who regularly gambled more and more extravagantly until he had lost all his money, were in some deeply emotional way congenial to me. I have always felt at ease with unintellectual working-class people, always been uneasy in the presence of typical Eton and Winchester, Oxford and Cambridge, products. A deplorably slapdash generalisation, I know, yet one conveying an essential truth about my lifelong desire (however inadequately fulfilled) not to be bound by an accent, a style, a code of manners, a way of eating food or wearing

45

clothes. Those Friday and Saturday nights spent in one or another dingy room of Battersea's back streets, which ended with me either skint or counting folding money, were among the happiest of my life.

*

Things go on together, but, without a conscious intention to deceive, one puts them down separately. If I have conveyed an impression of myself as a bohemian sportsman, that would be almost the reverse of the truth. When I closed the door of Jimmy Sharman's or Charlie Burgess's house, I walked up the hill to Clapham in the grey light of early morning, unlocked quietly the door of our house, crept noiselessly into bed. My mother rarely asked questions about where I had been. It was enough for her that I lived at home, and she only made a positive protest about my foolishness and ingratitude when I left at the age of twenty-four.

Things go on together: and what went on in my life was the daily journey by 26 or 28 tram to Victoria, the fingers tapping a typewriter in the service of Mr. Budette at the Victoria Lighting and Dynamo Company, the reading of books, the writing of poems, the dream of a literary magazine. To be as little educated as I was, to have left a state school at fourteen, may have compensations. It gave me a desperate desire to learn quickly what literature was about. Ignorance meant that I encountered great novels and poems with a shock of surprise that could never have been felt by anybody already sufficiently well-informed to know that Dostoevsky and Turgenev were not the same kind of novelist. The young man who worked away in the evening at improving his forehand drive, spent part of the day in discovering with astonishment the violent emotions not only felt but expressed by people in *The Brothers Karamazov*. Who would have supposed that Byron could be read like a novel, that Ben Jonson's plays were so funny, that you could get pleasure from Spenser without bothering about the symbolism? The lop-sided way in which I gained a literary education meant that everything I was able to appreciate came upon me with the force of a revelation. This characteristic endured for a long time. I can remember reading Boswell's Johnson just before the war, and forcing it on all my friends. Who would have dreamed that it could be anything but boring? Not ignoramuses like me.

Much of my unorganised reading was of modern literature, and it seems to me natural that this should have been so. I was surprised, when reading V. S. Pritchett's autobiography *Midnight Oil* recently, to learn that he lived in the Paris of Joyce, Hemingway and Scott Fitzgerald without ever having heard of them. I should have heard of them without doubt, I should have been hanging round the Dome as in fact when I was twenty-one I hung around the Wheatsheaf and the Fitzroy. Between the ages of seventeen and twenty-two I read *Ulysses*, Eliot's poems, Pound's early Cantos, Wyndham Lewis, any little magazines that I could buy cheaply. Much of what I read I did not understand, and often I looked for qualities that were not there. A book like *For Lancelot Andrewes* baffled me. I expected all "modern" writers to be revolutionary in language or attitude, but here was one talking about classicism, royalism, religion. What on earth did it mean? The poems, however, Eliot's and Pound's, and later Auden's, I understood better, and they opened up for me emotionally a miraculous world in which you could write about any subjects you liked in any tone of voice. I got back-numbers of *The Criterion* by sending a sixpenny stamp to Faber and Faber, bought the *Twentieth Century* and *New Verse* as they appeared, acquired a whole set of the defunct *Coterie* and *New Coterie*. In the V.L.D. office, during the intervals between typing letters and answering telephone calls about secondhand dynamos, I sketched out covers and contents pages for a magazine called *The Contemporary*, invented contributors, actually wrote some articles. I remember only one title: "T. S. Eliot, the Classical Romantic". I did not think of sending the articles to magazines. It was enough simply to have written them.

I suppose I am describing a prolonged adolescence, one lengthened by the failure to cut myself away until a late age from the close tentacles of our family life. These tentacles were tighter than most. After my father's death when I was seventeen, my mother's full strength of character emerged. To keep our heads financially above water she let rooms in our large Victorian house, kept accounts which recorded the spending of every penny. The three of us who lived at home, Maurice, my sister Edith and I, gave her money every week, but were still reminded often of the need for economy. At one time Maurice was out of work for nearly eighteen months,

48

and both he and my mother felt the act of signing on at a Labour Exchange, and inability to obtain a job, as a social stigma. My mother had no particular political views, although she voted Tory, but she felt strongly that those without jobs must in some way or other be blameworthy.

Yet she had two faces, two aspects. The cautious matriarch, full of phrases emphasising the virtues of timidity and obedience ("Cut your coat according to your cloth ... you've got to learn to walk before you can run ... all can't be masters, some must be men ... go to your room and put a padlock on your tongue"), was melted by the daring, recklessness, spontaneous generosity, of which in theory she disapproved. My father's possession of these qualities, or some of them, must have been what attracted her to him. She forgave him every extravagance, every hopeless speculation, happy in the knowledge that he would never obey her advice, and that he was a man who never put a padlock on his tongue. She managed to save some money that he knew nothing about, and put it into a Post Office account, but most of it had to be used when one or another of his schemes came to shipwreck. My brother A. J. had a capacity for extravagance that she publicly deplored, but secretly admired. She longed for the severely financial considerations by which she judged everything to be ignored. When I left home she warned me that I should find everything much more expensive living on my own. I should be eating out of tins, I should never cook for myself, it would be vital to my health that I came home for at least one good meal a week. She added two typically practical pieces of ad-

49

vice. "Be careful with shop-bought pies. Only buy Lazenby's tinned salmon."

We never escape from our childhood, but adolescence has its end. After leaving home I played no more serious table tennis (except that much later, in the Army, I won the regimental championship, my sole military distinction), no more cricket, no more snooker. The long nights spent at cards were finished. And I emancipated myself too from the influence of Maurice, my mentor in so many things when I was a boy. The family tentacles, now that I look back consideringly, gripped him even more firmly than they did me. Like my father, he had had the capacity for extravagant gestures. When they started a bookmaking business together, their small capital (his small capital, really) vanished like snow under arc lamps. Later he enormously enjoyed work as a bookmaker's clerk, particularly when he was on the course. But those eighteen months out of work, that came when the bookmaker cut down his staff because of the slump, affected him greatly. They brought out the caution inherited from my mother, and once he had found a job he never left it.

As the years passed we drifted apart from each other emotionally, the old jokes and catch phrases we had shared no longer seemed to me interesting or funny. When we met we did not have much to say to each other. As the coffin sank down to the furnace in Northampton crematorium I thought of the help and generosity he had shown me in the past, help upon the whole inadequately acknowledged or repaid. But the very closeness of our past relationship created a barrier between us. There is nothing we more consciously wish to forget than the trivialities—they can hardly be dignified with the word mistakes—of our adolescence.

A Glimpse of Thirties Sunlight

One day in the summer of 1935, a sunny day, the pavements gleaming, I sat in the Mitre Coffee House in Mitre Court just off Fleet Street, waiting for Geoffrey Grigson. The teashop was a kind of meeting place, just across from the *Morning Post* where he worked, to which he called young contributors to *New Verse* for inspection and consideration. I had sent him poems from time to time and they had been returned with what I came to recognise later as characteristic little notes. "These poems are interesting, but not interesting enough. They might be by Allen Tate, or XYZ," one note said. It seemed encouraging to be compared to Allen Tate, but if Tate was only equivalent to XYZ perhaps there was not much in it after all. Eventually Grigson accepted some poems, and invitations to tea followed.

Sometimes, but only occasionally, another young writer was present. My original vision of the teashop as a meeting place for young poets, a Fleet Street version of David Archer's Parton Bookshop, proved to be wide of the mark. It was a rather genteel establishment which served delicate little teacakes, and it was almost always empty.

Not on this occasion, however. In one corner of the shop sat two young men, one almost silent, the other a hatchet-faced figure wearing a large black hat who talked a great deal. "*Geoffrey Grigson*," Hatchet-face would say sometimes, like an exhausted swimmer calling for help, "Geoffrey Grigson says . . .". Brown eyes behind huge glasses under the black hat flashed meaningfully in my direction. I sipped my tea and waited without answering these signals, and in the end he had to ask outright: "Are you waiting for Geoffrey Grigson?" He introduced himself. His name was Ruthven Todd, he worked up in Edinburgh on a magazine called the *Scottish Bookman* and was down in London for a few days. His silent companion was a Scottish painter.

Grigson never turned up (in this respect the story is like that piece of Thurber's about not meeting D. H. Lawrence), and after sloughing off the painter Ruthven and I spent the evening drinking. He was staying in a Pimlico boarding house and at about midnight we decided that I should stay there too, sleeping on the floor. An hour later, heavy with drink, I staggered out into the Pimlico night to take in great gulps of air. On returning I found the house in darkness, tried several doors, found one that opened, and sank on to the floor. A man's voice said something.

"Is that Ruthven?"

The reply was brisk. "No, it's not Ruthven, and fuck off out of it."

The next unlocked door really was Ruthven's. He was in bed, smoking, and prepared to carry on our conversation at just the point where we had left it. In the morning I went off to work at V.L.D., with a bad headache, and Ruthven no doubt continued his round of talking and drinking before going back to Edinburgh. It may even be that he found Geoffrey Grigson.

The friendship so casually begun developed when later we lived on opposite sides of a Pimlico square. It has survived the stresses of more than thirty years: stresses which include the continuous flow of Ruthven's conversation, which I sometimes listen to disregardingly as if it were the lappings of the sea, and the serious strain placed upon it by the caricature of him in my first detective story.

I suppose it could fairly be said that Grigson's way of life was symbolised by the Mitre Coffee House and the *Morning Post*, to the extent at least that his habits were bourgeois and respectable, his clothes sedately smart. A sherry party at his flat in Keats Grove was not likely to develop into an orgy, or even into a literally highly intoxicating evening. He had no taste for literary bohemianism, which was represented at this time by the group of poets who were habitues of the Parton Bookshop, Dylan Thomas, George Barker and David Gascoyne among them. Later the bookshop was the focal point for contributors to *Contemporary Poetry and Prose* which was run by Roger Roughton, an aesthetic-looking young man with some literary tact and taste which were exhibited in his choice of contributions for the ten numbers of his magazine. The last issue, which appeared eighteen months after the first, carried a terminal notice admirable in its terseness: "This is the last number of *Contemporary Poetry and Prose*, as the Editor is going abroad for some time." I believe Roughton never returned to England. Early in 1941 he committed suicide in Dublin. In a letter to John Davenport suggesting some kind of memorial to him, Dylan Thomas commended "his work for the Communist Party, his publishing, his parties, himself". The Grigson and Roughton circles were distinctly different ones, although the same poets might be found writing in both magazines—Thomas, Gascoyne, Gavin Ewart, Kenneth Allott. There existed at this time a third poetic circle of a lower order, represented by the "Poet's Corner" in the *Sunday Referee*, and Victor Neuburg who ran it.

It is safe to say that there has been nothing like the Poet's Corner either before or since. Generally, three or four poems were printed in the paper each week and, rather in the style of a *New Statesman* competition, one was judged the best. It appeared in heavy type with some well-meant but often ludicrous editorial comment. "A perfect picture of life symbolised perfectly in footsteps", Neuburg wrote about a bad poem of mine, and of a poem printed in the same week he said that it was "another 'Life'-poem, the last two lines, especially, are of the quintessence of poetry". Sometimes his flights of language were more fanciful, like the use of "HeShe" to avoid the variation of sex in pronouns. The winner of each week's competition received half a guinea, and runners-up were given a miscellany of gifts ranging from propelling pencils and wallets to copies of Neuburg's own books. One of these, *Songs of the Groves* ("Records of the Ancient World"), was on my shelves for years, although it had vanished when I looked for it the other day. For his activities as editor of Poet's Corner Neuburg received the pittance of £2 a week.

It may seem strange that anybody took him seriously, but the prevailing poetic climate was such that young poets were pleased to find verse printed regularly anywhere at all. Today, when a concrete poem may appear in one of the Sunday papers or the *Times Literary Supplement*, and when editors are looking out eagerly for bright young men, it is difficult to imagine a time when it was a mark of audacity on the part of the literary editor of *The Listener*, Janet Adam Smith, to print what were were thought objectionably "modern" poems, and to use young poets occasionally as reviewers. Nowadays literary magazines proliferate, thanks largely to Arts Council subsidies: and while I wouldn't want to see any of those subsidies (well, hardly any) taken away, there was something good in the prewar situation. It was difficult to get poems printed, but perhaps now it is too easy. A certain toughness of attitude was engendered, which had its own virtue. To each generation its own rubbish, but more of it finds print now than then.

Anyway poets, Ruthven, Gascoyne, Thomas and Laurie Lee among them, did contribute to the *Sunday Referee* column and to the magazine *Comment* which Neuburg founded when a change of editorship meant that Poet's Corner was summarily stopped. A number of them went to the weekly meetings where he held court at a house in St. John's Wood, either to the Creative Circle he founded or to have tea in the garden on Sunday afternoon. I went to perhaps half a dozen of these meetings. A good deal has been written about Neuburg, about his infinite kindness and goodness (Pamela Hansford Johnson), his genius for drawing to himself trust and love by wisdom, graveness, humour and innocence (Dylan Thomas), and so on. No doubt he was a kind and gentle man (although it is easy to be kind to the young, especially when they admire you), but I must confess that he seemed to me like his writings primarily absurd. He was a gnome-like man with a large head, a sort of decayed Swinburne in appearance, with very fine clear blue eyes and a rotting nose. (A detail not produced by malice: it is mentioned by Arthur Calder-Marshall in his memoir of Neuburg.) His voice was high and lilting, and his manner like his appearance rather Swinburnian. He was borne upon waves of enthusiasm, darting as it were from the crest of one to the crest of another, and filling the spaces between with extraordinary jokes and old-fashioned slang. " 'Are you a FROG?' meant 'Are you a Friend Of God?), and the question might be followed by an invitation to 'Have a gasper". I can remember him asking whether I had read "The City of Dreadful Night" and refusing to accept the possibility that I could dislike such "a won-der-ful, won-der-ful poem".

He was undoubtedly a bohemian, and bohemianism was a condition I vaguely aspired to at the time, but there was also a vegetarian air about him, an atmosphere of date-and-banana sandwiches, which repelled me. I might have liked him better in the days of his youth, when he was prancing about performing magic rituals with Aleister Crowley and sleeping naked on a litter of gorse. All that, however, was a distant memory at the time of the Creative Circle, for his life at St. John's Wood was presided over by a stately, handsome lady who reminded me strongly of Margaret Dumont, stooge of the Marx Brothers. Margaret (she is called simply "the Lady" in a recent biography of Neuburg) was a strong believer in spare living and high thinking. She disapproved of alcohol, and refused to have it in the house, although a bottle of beer was smuggled in occasionally and Pamela Hansford Johnson records an evening when Margaret complained that she and Dylan Thomas had given the house over to "orgies and beer-gardens". It is likely that she regarded herself as saving Neuburg from bohemian ruin, as Watts-Dunton saved Swinburne.

I never saw Pamela Hansford Johnson or Dylan Thomas at St. John's Wood, although they were frequent attendants, and many of the other people gathered there seemed to me deplorable literary hangers-on. At one meeting, however, I met Herbert Mallalieu and Marjorie, who soon afterwards became his wife Mallalieu and I shared a taste not only for drink but for cricket—an interest in sport was not fashionable among the 'thirties literati as it is today—and for playing elaborate games. There was an empty room in the flat they lived in at Croydon, and I moved into it. The room on the landing opposite me was occupied first by Derek Savage, another young poet, and later by an actor named Ernest Clark.

I talked to Herbert and Derek about my idea of starting a magazine. No doubt we had in mind getting our own poems printed, but there was a real difference of attitude then between poets who had been to a university, like Auden, Spender, MacNeice, Day Lewis, Empson, Lehmann, and those who hadn't, like Thomas, Barker, Ruthven, Roy Fuller, and the three of us. There was a whole range of subjects from which we were cut off and about which most of them wrote, but also they seemed to have a common tone as of friends talking to each other in a way that excluded strangers. I don't think I would try to justify this feeling today, I merely note its existence at the time. Probably it was nurtured by the heavy dependence of *New Verse* on Auden. Anyway we decided—or I decided, since neither Herbert nor Derek had any spare money, while I was able to save a few pounds from the wage I was paid at V.L.D.—to start a magazine. In the end Derek had little to do with it, but Herbert and his wife helped with the donkey work, the five hundred circulars optimistically sent out that brought nine subscriptions, the copies sent or taken to bookshops, typing and filling envelopes, packing parcels. In our spare time Herbert and I played a very good indoor cricket game called Stumpz.

"H. B. Mallalieu", a poet now well known said to me the other day, "I remember in my youth I used to be quite excited to see that name in a magazine." Neither Mallalieu nor Savage survived the war as poets, and indeed I have the impression that the number of emotional casualties among young 'thirties poets was exceptionally high. Both were published in volume form by the

Fortune Press, which was run single-handed by a man named Caton from a basement room in Buckingham Palace Road. Caton's primary interest was in quite a different kind of literature, made evident by the books piled high in his windowless room—*Boy Sailors*, *True Yokefellow* and *Fourteen, a diary of the Teens*, by a Boy, were typical of them. There was, as he said, no money in poetry, but still he printed first volumes by a good many young poets of the time, including Fuller, Ewart, Francis Scarfe, George Woodcock. Apart from one case, that in which he bought the copyright of Thomas's *Eighteen Poems* outright for only £15 according to Thomas's biographer, he paid no money to his authors and even to write of them being "on his list" would be misleading, because he issued no list. I was never able to find out how many copies he printed of each book he produced, but I suppose several of them are rarities now. Perhaps there was a little money in poetry for Caton after all. I hope so. The fact that poets agreed so readily to Catonic publishing shows again how limited were the possibilities open to them. It was the belief of some writers that he never read their work, although this was rather contradicted by his saying to me about Gavin Ewart's *Poems and Songs:* "This fellow Ewart now, he's rather spicy, eh?"

Apart from his liking for spiciness Caton had no particular literary tastes or opinions, and he later published *The White Horseman*, the anthology by those Apocalyptic poets who ushered in the woolly 'forties and swamped the commonsensible minor 'thirties writers. He was, I think, a little astonished to find that anybody took his

Fortune poets seriously. When Tambimuttu attacked my poems he wrote to me- "The review of your poems seems rather offensive—is the reviewer the brown fellow?"

To go back in detail over the history of *Twentieth Century Verse*, the little magazine I started with Herbert Mallalieu's help, as it followed me for three years from Croydon to Pimlico and then to Clapham, would be an exercise in boredom for readers, but looking over some correspondence which Herbert has recently unearthed, I see that my letter-writing style had at that time an unexpectedly Poundian flavour. "Play this on your victrola and tell me what you think of it . . . the last two verses of your poem seem to abandon the Dowley Cunne and Ramvell stile . . . Mallalieu on SATIRE should be a FAIR BUGGAR... You should be CAREFUL of Ackerley... IT IS NOT POSSIBLE now to write good verse in the manner of

Love, too, has changed, who sees its limits drawn
So far below the wished eternity.

It is against lines like these that I say (or Mr Smith says) bang bang. . . . If we print 1500 copies and only *sell* 700 we shall stand a good chance of busting up, if we print 750 copies we shall make a certain profit. There's a *Poetry and the People* party next Friday, they talk about their Mayakovsky punch."

The financial calculations refer to Herbert's persuasive skill in getting several advertisements for one number, but who was Mr. Smith? I don't remember. And, as always happens in reading old correspondence, I found things that startled me, like an offhand remark: "I think perhaps I am going to be married. But not yet. And anyway it is a matter for condolence, not congratulation." The girl in question was a White Russian Jewess who had sent me a sonnet beginning:

Love is thick, wet, warm, sticky, and it hurts.

I did not print this or her other poems, but I did meet the girl, and we became lovers. Memory is deeply untrustworthy. I would have sworn that I had never mentioned this brief intention of getting married to anybody.

One or two aspects of the magazine have some literary-historical interest. In comparing the English poetic scene of the 'thirties with that at the present time, the thing that impresses me most is our parochialism and ignorance. John Lehmann opened the pages of *New Writing* to a number of European writers but there was no general understanding of what (for instance) Brecht represented and was trying to do, and I remember being overwhelmed by the icy Marxist liveliness of *A Penny for the Poor*. The American revolution in poetic language that had begun in 1912 was not known to us in any detail, and most modern American poets were represented in England by a few anthology pieces. Stevens was "Le Monocle de Mon Oncle" or "The Emperor of Ice-Cream", and nothing else. American criticism was even less known, and I do not suppose there were more than a few dozen people who had read John Crowe Ransom's *The World's Body* or Yvor Winters's *Primitivism and Decadence*.

Ignorance is always a defect, and yet as I have suggested earlier it can be a blessing too. A firm ignorance of what
62

was poetically fashionable helped to give the early poems of Dylan Thomas and George Barker their freshness and originality. Even for editors, particularly of little magazines, ignorance has its usefulness. Few magazines are so dull as those run in the service of an easily pleased eclecticism. Ignorance led me to passionate championing of some dud poets, but that is an occupational error of editors. Among the many embarrassing pages of *Twentieth Century Verse* there are some in which what still seem to be genuine poems appear:

> All day from the east slanted snow
> Covering pavement toys and the metal men
> Who speak for England the lead laws of ago.

The *tone* of lines like these which begin George Woodcock's "Snow" is specifically English, unAudenic, and again the product of ignorance in the sense that if at this time Woodcock had known the work of the best modern Americans he would have been a different, less direct and ingenuous writer. It would be possible to make a little anthology of poetry written during the 'thirties which owed the smallest possible debt to Auden or Thomas, and yet was permanently interesting as the product of something truly seen and experienced. Woodcock, Savage, Ruthven Todd, Kenneth Allott, would certainly feature prominently in such a collection, as well as writers now totally forgotten.

Little magazines in England had smaller circulations then than they have today, but it seems to me that they had more influence. An appearance in *New Verse* would certainly have seemed important to any young poet, and by avoidance of the literary matiness that is about at any time both Grigson and I gathered enemies, some in unsuspected places. "Glad your first article (about Thomas's poetry) was disliked by Grigson and Symons", Thomas wrote to his acolyte Henry Treece, and to Tambimuttu after the first issue of his *Poetry* (London): "Poetry editors are mostly vicious climbers, with their fingers in many pies, their eyes at many keyholes, and their tongues at many bottoms." The remark seems a curious one to make about people who had committed no sin worse than to print his poems and lend him money: but of course it was prompted by the temperamental dislike Thomas felt for editors who were choosy, commented and criticised, were uninfluenced by an Old Pals' Act or a boozy evening on the town: editors very much unlike the amiable irresponsible open-armed Tambimuttu. The characteristics Grigson and I had in common, which largely ordered the tone of our magazines, were amusingly analysed by Hugh Gordon Porteus in a contemporary article:

Both, significantly, are youngest sons in large families with a respectable Victorian background. Both are "concerned"—feel responsible about—"the situation" and "poetry" (in that order). Both are proof against the grosser and more manifest deceits of the day. . . . Both are owlish and bespectacled, like BOP swots grown prefectorial. Both enjoy the roles of patron and district magistrates. Both bark more (even) than they bite. As dictators G. would approximate to the Cripps model, J. to de Valera. G. belongs

64

to the order of autocratic Cornish giants, auntsallied by the slings and arrows of the minuscular: J. suggests one of DHL's "long-nosed, heavy-footed, subtly-smiling Etruscans" as much as anything.

Such an article (I have quoted only a fragment from Porteus's eight pages) is interesting as a proof of the parochialism I have been talking about. What magazine today would print such a piece about district magistrates? I had better disclaim any idea that by linking my name with Grigson's I am suggesting that our activities were of anything like equal importance. *New Verse* was and remains in almost every way a model of what a small verse magazine should be. (Of course, it was lucky that Auden happened to be around.) *Twentieth Century Verse* improved a great deal after an unhappy first year but, partly because of the self-denying ordinance that excluded big names, it never did more than palely reflect *New Verse's* virtues. Well, perhaps a little more by encouraging the young poets I have mentioned, but not very much.

In the summer of 1939 what proved to be the last numbers of both magazines appeared. With the war the world of rational intelligence and close observation on which they had been based seemed to vanish almost overnight, to be replaced poetically by the triumphant *Poetry*, "a vast junk shop, or oriental bazaar, in which you may pick up—among the curios—odd bargains, simple pots, and genuine Birmingham brass", as Porteus put it. And in any case, little as it cost to run a magazine in those days, I could no longer afford to pay the gap

C

between the printer's bill and the receipts. If there was no room for two magazines, should we make them one? The suggestion came from Geoffrey—we were by this time on first-name terms—who was also, I think, feeling the financial strain of running a magazine, and we discussed the possibilities at length but indecisively over two lunches at the Café Royal. "He insisted on talking about ART, Josh Reynolds and William Etty and William Coldstream and all those chaps", I reported to a friend, I am sure somewhat inaccurately. I can't now remember just what course the conversations took, but I do recall that Geoffrey was eager to look at my subscription list so that he could see how far it coincided with that of *New Verse*, and that I was reluctant to reveal it. I think also that I didn't care much for the implication that he would edit the new or joint magazine and that I should be his assistant. But our conversations never reached a point sufficiently advanced to find us really in disagreement. Very soon Geoffrey was writing to me of a general gloom which enveloped him, and of being "not impotent exactly, but inorgiastic". The reference was sexual, but by extension referred to "the situation" as well, a situation offering no room for optimism. As far as I know, he gave up the attempt to continue *New Verse*, and I gave up too, publishing the poems I had on hand in a rather good little pamphlet called "Some Poems in Wartime". A note in my London Letter for *Kenyon Review* in December 1939, provided a coda for the whole thing:

The *New Verse Anthology*, published at the end of August, now reads like a valediction: the end of *New*

Verse is the end, for this time, of the movement towards commonsense standards in English letters. It is axiomatic that "commonsense" has little chance in a war: and it is obvious too that inflation of language and sentiment in literature is as certain in wartime as inflation of prices. . . . It is not difficult to see what will happen in the near future. The emotional temperature will go up, poetry and prose will become more "poetic", Eliot's just remark that "poetry is nearer to 'verse' than it is to prose poetry" will be forgotten. . . .

In time, and not very much time, all these things came to pass. It was no time for commonsense editors.

So that was the end of it. Well, not quite the end. Behind the serious, the ludicrous always lurks. In November 1939, there appeared a curious new magazine called *Kingdom Come*. The editor was an undergraduate named John Waller and the magazine had a sub-head, "The Magazine of War-time Oxford", later changed to "Founded in War-time Oxford". *Kingdom Come*, rechristened by me *Condom King*, had a format rather larger than that of *Encounter* and an atrociously ugly neo-expressionist cover design. Its contents were an extraordinary ragbag, including poems and articles by undergraduates, poems by Marie Stopes and Lord Alfred Douglas, stories by H. E. Bates and Kay Boyle, Philip Toynbee's account of being cut by a Party member after writing a letter to the *New Statesman* about the invasion of Finland—but also poems and criticism by many refugees from the 'thirties magazines, including Geoffrey on "The Present State of English Poetry" and some pieces of mine. It is impossible to convey the rich confusion of *Kingdom Come*: I doubt if any odder magazine has appeared since its extinction after eight issues.

At this time Waller left England for service overseas, and I was asked if I would take over the editorship. The money backing the magazine had been provided by Marie Stopes, whose sonnet to Churchill had been printed:

> The face that women horsewhipped long ago
> Now lashes women through the Bevin scourge
> That armaments, not men, our girls must make.

Would Dr. Stopes approve of me as editor? And would she expect her own peoms to be printed? A reply paid telegram arrived: "Coming to London Wednesday can you lunch with me Ritz. Stopes". I reported on the occasion in a letter:

> The lunch was disappointingly inexpensive, the whole thing, with a bottle of wine (which I drank— Marie is TT) came to 17/6. Birth control's Sylvia Pankhurst looks like a rather homely washerwoman, red-necked and broad-bosomed. . . . "Wine," she said to me, "What sort of wine will you have—I don't know much about that sort of thing. I only know one wine—Madeira. I have a cellar full of Madeira."

She agreed to go on backing *Kingdom Come* with me as editor, and made no stipulations about her own work. But my hopes of surviving in wartime without either going into prison as a conscientious objector or into the forces grew thinner each day. Within a few weeks I was in Birmingham working in a factory in an attempt to escape the draft. My erratic progress left no time for editorial work, and if there had been time, were enough poems being written that I should have wanted to print? In a small way such a magazine as *Twentieth Century Verse* was an image of its time, and with the fading of the 'thirties' sunlight that time was over.

Our Friend, Cyril Y. Snaggs

The epithet *our friend* is now rarely heard, but in my youth it was common among certain kinds of business men. Certainly it was often used by Mr. Budette, my employer at Victoria Lighting and Dynamo, and his acquaintances. It meant something the reverse of friendly. If somebody was cutting up rough, as Mr. Budette would typically put it, about trouble on a machine we had sold to them, he would come back from our nearby pub the Albert and say, "Our friend needs a little lesson in manners". When one of our suppliers thought that he could charge us more than the original estimated price for some repair work, our friend had another think coming. If somebody was dunning us for a long overdue bill, our friend had to be taught that money did not grow on trees. After our friend had been made to see reason, generally by means of a genially abusive telephone call, he was at least temporarily removed from the offending

70

category. Only one man I have known invoked *our friend* more often than Mr. Budette, and this was Cyril Y. Snaggs.

He came into my life at the beginning of the war when the always uncertain financial position of V.L.D. became not desperate but undoubtedly difficult. The trade in secondhand motors and dynamos fell away almost to nothing, although it recovered a little later on. It was impossible to obtain any more of the German-made Puyrelite Lighting Fittings for which we held the sole agency, and the most grandiose of Mr. Budette's achemes for making money quickly, the Pimlico Clinic for the electrical treatment of hay fever by ionizing the nasal membranes, ended when the operator employed at the Clinic disappeared. We discovered after he had gone that this operator, a slightly intellectual Jewish Fascist who had left the British Union of Fascists when they became openly anti-Semitic, had induced a number of clients to give him personal cheques for long courses of treatment. Indignant hay fever victims threatened to sue the Clinic and Mr. York, who had put up the money for it, paid back some of the fees and closed down the enterprise. Mr. Budette, sitting opposite me in the big V.L.D. office which we shared after York's departure (I had been promoted to it from the windowless cubby hole I originally occupied) said, as he had often said to me before, "We must have a new régime, Symons. We've got to make a change."

We made a change. The remainder of the Puyrelite fittings were put up in the attic, and the showroom that had housed them was let to another electrical firm run by a mouldering colonel whose business had slumped even more drastically than that of V.L.D. Mr. Budette's master-stroke, however, was in letting the crane room to Cyril Y. Snaggs, who had been appointed the London manager of Midlands Paint Sprayers, a Birmingham firm who had decided that they needed a base in London. The crane room had in better days been used for storing dynamos, which were pulled up from the street. Now the crane was dismantled and the room painted. Spraying machines and cabinets replaced the dynamos in the workshop below. An impressive brass plate appeared on the shabby entrance. It was agreed that I should work not only for V.L.D. and the mouldering colonel but for Midlands Paint Sprayers too. Mr. Budette and I both made rather a good thing out of it. Everybody, at first, was happy.

Cyril Y. Snaggs (the Y stood for Yeatman, a family name) was a burly man with patches of red on his cheeks that might have been painted there, a horse's wide nostrils through which he blew angrily or eagerly, a large box mouth in which false teeth emphatically clicked, and hairy capable hands. His voice was loud, his manner choleric, his handshake painfully firm. He gripped my hand at our first meeting and said that he would be relying on me for all the help I could give him. Mr. Budette had told him about my registration as a conscientious objector and also about the verse magazine that I edited mostly in office time, and he seemed to feel that in some mysterious way the two activities cancelled out each other "I tell you frankly, I detest your politics," he said with what I came to know as a characteristic glare. "We
72

won't talk about them, if you don't mind, least said soonest mended." Then he went on to say something about understanding that people mixed up with poetry were a funny lot and that it was not his business anyway. "We'll be working in harness, got to pull together. If we make a team we'll get on."

Snaggs was in his middle forties, one of Mr. Budette's drinking companions at the Albert. He had had a dozen jobs of one kind and another in the years before the war, all of them as a salesman. I never found out how somebody with no administrative experience had landed this job with Midlands Paint Sprayers—perhaps his downright manner impressed them at an interview—but he started out with immense energy to get the London office established. A stream of applicants came in for the post of travelling representative and two were taken on the payroll. They were known by their initials—Snaggs was a great man for initials, which he equated with brisk efficiency—as L. P. U. and G. W. Enquiries, requests for catalogues, and then orders ensued. I was busier than I had ever been in the V.L.D. days, and Snaggs clicked away in satisfaction at the system I evolved for separating one area from another, cataloguing clients, using different colour cards for enquiries, follow ups, service calls, orders, complaints. Head Office expressed approval, clearly we were making a team.

Such smooth progress delighted Snaggs in a way, but it did not satisfy him emotionally. Metaphysical fire was always shooting out of his nostrils, he was a quarrelsome man who needed an enemy. He found one soon enough in the director we dealt with in Birmingham, a man

73

named Jenkins, who wrote memoranda in what he obviously thought a highly literary style. We would receive notes reading: "In reply to your memo 181 B anent delivery to Southern Factors, we are doing our best but this line is out of stock and in present conditions I fear a diuturnity may elapse before maturation is possible." Snagg's irritation at receiving such notes was reasonable, his expression of it excessive. We had no telex to Birmingham, and telephone calls from London were not encouraged except on urgent matters, but Snaggs was on the line in a moment asking how long a diuturnity lasted and whether maturation had anything to do with maternity. Afterwards he would click his teeth at me, breathing hard as though he had just won a race. "I think we showed our friend just where he got off, Symons, eh?" Within a short time he was on such bad terms with Jenkins that I handled most of the calls from Head Office direct. "It's that man again," Snaggs would say, and add without bothering to put his hand over the telephone receiver: "Little Hitler. Talk to him, will you?"

His relations with L. P. U. also deteriorated quickly G. W. was mild-mannered and totally harmless, but L. P. U., a hard-drinking red nosed traveller of the old school was always difficult to reach at home with urgent messages, rarely 'phoned in, and sometimes even failed to attend the Thursday travellers' conference at which calls were arranged for the following week. When Snaggs did reach him on the telephone he would ask, in a tone heavy with sarcasm, whether L. P. U. could spare time to look in at the office. Occasionally L. P. U., a man not easily put down and insusceptible to sarcasm, would say that he was too busy, and then Snaggs would roar: "I want to see you. Tomorrow at ten thirty. Is that clear?" Slamming down the telephone he would say to me: "Our friend's got to learn that he can't do that there 'ere." L.P.U. would arrive, red nosed and cheerful, and the quarrel would be resolved by a drinking session.

Snaggs's attitude towards me was one of slightly embarrassing friendliness faintly tinged with hostility. I got on very well with Mr. Budette, but in the ten years of our acquaintance he had never invited me to his house in Upper Norwood, nor had I expected him to do so. I had never even attended one of the Albert drinking lunches. I regarded secretarial work as something I had to do to make money, and it was utterly unrelated in my mind to the "real world" of evenings and week-ends in which I went to political meetings, drank, talked about art, met girls. Perhaps such dissociation was a bad thing, but at the time it seemed to me part of the natural order. Most of my friends engaged in some sort of pseudo-literary work like journalism or advertising to make a living, I was a secretary instead, it seemed to me as simple as that. I was surprised when one day Snaggs invited me to dinner at his house, and distinctly disconcerted to find that I had been asked not in my business capacity but as a writer (even though Snaggs had read nothing I had written), conscientious objector, holder of heretical opinions. We drove out one evening to his bungalow at Sanderstead. There I found again with surprise, although this is the kind of shock to which I have long since become inured, that Snaggs too had a public and a private face.

Mrs. Snaggs was a dainty little lady of great gentility, and the bungalow was dainty too. In her presence Snaggs the roarer was a sucking dove. She gently reproved him for offering spirits before dinner, saying that she was sure Mr. Symons would sooner have a glass of sherry. During the meal he was constantly up and about, taking dishes to the kitchen, offering to help, being criticised for the inefficiency of his carving. While we ate she plied me lightly with questions about the latest novels she had got from the local Boots' or Smith's libraries, and I could feel my status sinking as I said that I had read none of them. Things brightened up a little when she touched on my conscientious objection. "Cyril doesn't approve, but I told him that he must try to understand." She spoke of her unusually silent husband as though he were not there. "I think all war is very hateful, very terrible," Snaggs broke in at this to ask what would happen if everybody took that attitude, did she want Hitler to trample all over us? Mrs. Snaggs looked to me for a gesture of solidarity, but I was unable to make it. What would have been the point of explaining that my objections were political, that I believed only a near-Fascist government could successfully oppose Fascism, and opposed the war in the name of a revolution which would sweep away all Snaggses and their bungalows?

Later Snaggs and I played chess, his moves punctuated by grunts and clicks, while Mrs. Snaggs first cleared away, and then maintained mild conversation with me. The uneasy evening came to an end which I might have foreseen when she produced a sheaf of her poems and asked me to take them away and give me a frank opinion of their merits. In vain I said that my little magazine had been suspended for the duration. The poems were pressed on me, and I departed with them. I cannot remember what they were like, or what anodyne words I wrote to her. Snaggs never referred to the visit afterwards, but there was some change in his manner towards me. The evening marked the high point of our relationship, which afterwards steeply declined.

The decline was marked by an absurd incident. Mr. Budette was a good-natured man, but he felt an affinity for failure rather than success, and found it natural to view business as a battle of wits rather than an affair of effortful striving. He was himself what he sometimes called a self-made man, and Snaggs's frequent references to his prep school and minor public school annoyed him. The Colonel, as he once said to Snaggs, had been at Eton but didn't make a bloody song and dance about it. Beyond this he was irritated by Snaggs's boastfully busy manner, and by his success in setting up the London office. Mr. Budette must unconsciously have compared this success with the declining fortunes of V.L.D., which existed at this time on orders for electric lamps and other odds and ends given us by firms like Watney Combe Reid. In these transactions he acted simply as a middleman, taking his discount merely for passing on an order. I had far more work to do for Midlands Paint Sprayers than for V.L.D. and the Colonel combined, and this annoyed him too.

"I tell you what our friend Snaggs is made of," he said. "Piss and wind, he's all piss and wind." Returning one day from the Albert in company with the Colonel he asked me to tell Snaggs that an outside call had come through, and then connect the two of them through our internal switchboard. Using an undefined regional accent quite unlike his own voice, Mr. Budette then played the role of a disatisfied client. Snaggs loved the telephone and was proud of his technique in dealing with customers, but irascibility soon replaced his "Can we be of service to you?" manner under the stress of what was in effect personal abuse.

"I've been on to your Mr. Jenkins and he told me to get in touch with you", Mr. Budette said. "I told him your machines won't work, they're no bloody good."

"Very sorry to hear you're having trouble," Snaggs replied. "Our aim is to give service. Just tell me where you are, I'll get a man along immediately."

"He told me to ask for Cyril Y. Snaggs."

"Snaggs speaking."

"And I said to him, Snaggs I said, we've got enough snags already, is he like his name? And he said, I wouldn't be surprised."

Teeth clicked. "Who is that speaking, I didn't get the name."

Mr. Budette rattled off something unintelligible. "I told Jenkins, if he's no better than his stupid name I don't want him messing about with my equipment."

"What is your name?" Snaggs shouted.

"It won't be Snaggs who looks at your machines, Jenkins said, confidentially he doesn't know his arse from his elbow, but we've got some qualified engineers."

"*Jenkins said that*?" False teeth clattered like a monkey's.

78

The encounter went on for another couple of minutes and ended with Snaggs slamming down the receiver. He rushed in to tell Mr. Budette about the call, found the three of us helpless with laughter, and realised what had happened. His relationship with Mr. Budette was restored after a couple of days, but I remained unforgiven. "I shan't forget this," he said, and he never did. Rather more strangely, the incident exacerbated his feelings against Jenkins, as though he really had been responsible for the words attributed to him.

But Snaggs's star was in the descendant. Jenkins came down from Birmingham, and was not pleased by what he found. He was a short-haired, brisk executive, whose appearance could not at all be reconciled with those wordy memos. He had a couple of drinks in the Albert, but then made it clear that it was time to leave and get back to work. He thought quite rightly that the rent paid for the crane room was altogether excessive (I always suspected that Mr. Budette had made some typical private deal by which a percentage of the rent went to Snaggs), expressed dissatisfaction with the service given to customers by the travellers, said he wanted a twice-weekly report on paper of all London activities, and talked vaguely about taking a larger London office. The warning signs were clear, but Snaggs refused to read them. He embarked on long drinking bouts with Mr. Budette, the Colonel and others, which began at the Albert and continued in clubs, so that often he was out during the whole afternoon, returning at five o'clock purplish and breathing hard through distended nostrils. "What does the little tyke want now?" he would ask, reading with

79

glazed eyes a memo from Birmingham. The air raids on London had begun, and I thought of him staggering home to the ladylike little woman in Sanderstead. Did they go down to sleep in the air raid shelter when the bombs started to fall? Somehow I could not imagine it.

A few days later the blow fell. Snaggs was told that a new and larger office had been found just round the corner in Victoria Street, and that Mr. F. G. R. Remnant would be coming down from Birmingham to take charge of it. The firm greatly appreciated the help Snaggs had given in setting up London office, but felt that travelling representation ought to be increased and suggested that he should cover the London area, thus joining L. P. U. and G. W. and become C. Y. S. The letter was signed by the managing director, but Snaggs rightly saw in it Jenkins's vile hand. The news can't exactly have been unexpected, and in a sense he had provoked a struggle which he could only lose, but he took it very hard. To my surprise he accepted the demotion from Cyril Y. Snaggs, London Manager, to C. Y. S., London rep, but he blamed almost everybody involved, in particular Jenkins and me.

Blame for me was universal. Jenkins had rung Mr. Budette from Birmingham and arranged that I should spend four days a week working for them and one for him, and that they would pay the whole of my wages. Mr. Budette also squeezed three months' rent from them as notice for leaving the crane room. The whole arrangement was financially profitable to him, and convenient too, but he felt cheated by it, rather as though Midlands Paint Sprayers and I had combined to put over on him some extremely sharp deal. I think he felt that I was in a way his property, and that four-fifths of this property has been stolen from him. This feeling was somehow deepened by the fact that I was a conscientious objector and that Remnant, the new manager, was a dapper mild-mannered liberal who felt considerable sympathy for anybody trying to avoid military service. "I don't mind telling you that you're absolutely indispensable to our war effort," he said to me with a wink in Mr. Budette's presence. Snaggs, who had come to detest me almost as much as he hated Jenkins, expressed his feelings openly as he had never done before by saying: "They're going to catch up with all you bloody conchies soon."

We moved into the new offices, which were by the standards of the time luxurious. A girl typist was engaged. Memos flowed, business flourished. Bombing continued. Against the developing pattern of the war, threatened invasion, tightened belts, a sharpening of patriotic propaganda, Snaggs moved towards his doom.

Remnant was an easygoing man, able to get on with anybody, but the arrangement with Snaggs was hopeless from the start. Looking back, I can see that he must have taken on the humiliating job as rep only because he had become almost unemployable. He would have found life difficult enough under war conditions anyway, because he was essentially a salesman and the firm's work became more and more that of suppliers to various Forces departments, with the rep's role confined to giving advice on the installation and operation of the paint sprayers. More important than this, however, was his reluctance to admit that he was under Remnant's authority. He would arrive half-cut at the weekly conference and sit in the room's most comfortable chair, breathing heavily and shifting the glare of his slightly bulging eyes from the harmless G. W. to L. P. U., who had now become in a way his ally, and then turning the glare full strength on to Remnant and to me. His reports were vague, and full of abuse about the stupidity and slackness of the people he had to deal with. "They don't know there's a war on," he would say about the civilians at factories. "Somebody ought to put a bomb up their backsides." After making his report he would slump back in his chair and take no further active interest in the proceedings, answering Remnant's questions with irrelevances, and making the inadequacy of his petrol ration an excuse for failing to call on customers.

Mr. Budette, who now spent much more time in the V.L.D. office because in his absence it was left empty, and characteristically taught himself touch typing so that he could answer letters, tried without success to induce Snaggs to cut down on drinking. Remnant, who felt sorry for him, managed for a while to conceal his inefficiency from Birmingham, but in the end covering up became impossible. He arrived blind drunk to demonstrate the use of a paint sprayer at a government factory, connected a machine wrongly so that the motor burned out, and then blamed the manager. The manager told Remnant that they would not have him on the premises again and made a written complaint to Birmingham. Had Jenkins been expecting, planning for, such an outcome? Anyway, he was sacked at once.

I saw him for the last time when he came up to the

office to hand over his papers. He was pale except for those red spots on his cheeks, sober, restrained. He shook my hand with his painful grip and wished me luck. Remnant took him out to a lunch at which he refused alcohol and said that he hoped the firm would give him another chance, speaking of turning over new leaves. They refused.

There were no more leaves left for him to turn. A month later he died, not by enemy action nor as a suicide, but of a heart attack while driving to an appointment for a new job. Mr. Budette attended the funeral. Midlands Sprayers sent a wreath.

I think of them all now sometimes, of the Colonel whose business died of inanition, of Mr. Budette who managed somehow to survive the war with V.L.D. intact and then (his last triumph!) to sell the firm's goodwill at a handsome price, and of Snaggs. They seem to me fabulous figures. Are there still such people in business today, hard-drinking men proud of their suburban respectability but living from stratagem to stratagem, moving from job to job? I have the feeling that there would be no place for them nowadays. Even in his own time Cyril Y. Snaggs, with all his bounce and bluster and pretence, was a lost man in a hostile world.

How We Lost the War

September 7, 1940. Armageddon Day.

On this Saturday afternoon Roy Fuller and I went swimming in Brockwell Park. From a hill in the park we watched the tiny birds far overhead in the blue sky, dozens of them moving in formation undisturbed by the coughing tubes that puffed smoke around them. Very soon the crump of bombs sounded from the East End, and more flights of birds swam across the sky. The destruction of London had begun. It was a fulfilment of the prophecies we had been making for years, and there was nothing to be done about it. We went back to the house in Denmark Hill where I was living, and from there just a few steps up the road to a pub called The Fox Under the Hill, where we drank and played bar skittles until closing time.

The conditions in which I lived at Denmark Hill (Roy, who was awaiting call up, had come over for the day) seem now distinctly curious, but at the time I did not think there was anything unusual about them. The house, a largish white square Victorian villa opposite Ruskin Park, belonged to a dentist named Strong who had moved his wife and family out of London, returning only occasionally to see patients in his surgery. No doubt it was natural enough that Mr. Strong should have let his empty house, but how did he come to let it to a nest of political dissidents, the most active of whom were engaged in working against Britain's war interests? No doubt Rita was responsible. Bright and pretty as a penny, less than five feet tall even when she tottered in high heels, short-legged as a peasant, sharp-eyed and chirpily sexy, Rita was a constant source of fascination to Mr. Strong. He could be found lurking in the kitchen where she bustled about cooking delicate little dishes and looking roguishly at him while she sang at the top of her light voice a parody of a popular song:

> See the pretty lady up on the tree,
> The higher up the sweeter she grows.
> Picking fruit you've got to be
> *Up on your toes.*

Smiling shyly Mr. Strong the dentist would invite her to have a drink. In the billiards room he uncorked bottles, poured substantial tots of whisky or gin and, staring intently at her, proposed some toast like "Here's to peace" or "To the day when the lights go on again". "Bottoms up", Rita would respond with a giggle, and perhaps another drink would be poured. Reporting these sessions afterwards Rita would say: "I do believe he fancies me,

85

you know—the other day in there I was all of a quiver".
But she knew and we knew that Mr. Strong would
never really *do* anything. He was a married man himself,
for one thing. For another he believed that Rita was
married to Rex, and Mr. Strong was slightly awed by
Rex. He would chat easily enough with Lionel and me,
who made up the rest of the household, but in the
presence of Rex he was tongue-tied.

Rex was rather imperial in appearance, in a lean hungry
way. He was tall and fair, with a large impressive head
and a broken nose that gave him an air of toughness.
About all his movements, the gestures of his well-kept
thin hands, the way in which he straddled in front of a
fireplace, even the air with which he sat in a chair with
one leg crossed over the other knee, there was a misleadingly aristocratic air of negligent ease—misleading
because Rex was a working-class product who before
I knew him had worked as an insurance clerk. When I
first met him he had been living with Rita for some time.
(Both were married, with discarded wife and husband
vaguely in the background.) She had a small independent
income, and provided for his material needs while he
advanced the cause of world revolution. Rex, like the
rest of the household, was a Trotskyist, opposed to the
war and eager to overthrow the government.

His enthusiasm for political work varied. He would
sit furiously writing for half a day to produce a piece
showing that war could be fought successfully only
under workers' control of the armed forces, help to
duplicate the article and roll off the cyclostyled sheets
produced by Joe, a factory worker in the movement,
86

and then take an active part in distributing them. But when two or three such bits of propaganda had no effect Rex would become disheartened and lie about the house all day, making love to Rita or talking about Britain's inevitable defeat. Any small piece of news, a miners' strike in Wales or rumours of opposition to the war in the army, would cheer him up again, however, for he was by nature an optimist.

"God, Julian, if only we could have held off the war for another six months, we might have done something," he would say. But what could we have done? "Taken over. My God, in the factories we're gaining ground all the time. If we'd had another six months we could have called strikes everywhere, paralysed the war effort." Rex s voice, which should have been deep and rich, was in fact light, high, excitable. He shook his head and smiled at my disbelieving look. "I m afraid you re a cynic. Do you know how many active Bolsheviks there were in 1914? A few hundred. We've got two hundred and fifty. And we're growing."

The German invasion of Norway had cheered Rex up greatly because he thought that any extension of the war made the overturn of existing régimes more likely. The assassination of Trotsky in August cast him down for a week, until he realised that the Fourth International was not dead, but only the Old Man who had inspired it. Early in 1940 Rex had been forced to take a job, and he joined Camberwell A.R.P. It gave, he said, splendid opportunities for propaganda. The fire service were a progressive lot.

If Rex was a classic type of revolutionary dreaming

optimist, Lionel provided an overwhelming corrective to him. Where Rex, except on gloomy days, saw the victory of the working class as inevitable, this was for Lionel a prospect so distant as to be invisible. What really could be done, except to prepare for the illegal struggles ahead in a few months' time under German occupation? All Lionel's revolutionary writing, and he did a good deal of it, was under pseudonyms, and he was never associated with the distribution of literature in the street. As a member of the local Borough Council he carried out a persistent campaign of sniping at the established Labour group which won him a small reputation, so that he was able occasionally to publise a minor local scandal of bureaucratic incompetence. He did not overestimate the importance of this. "Doesn't really mean anything," he would say. "Bloody hopeless, the British. They won't even stand in queues properly." The irresponsibility of the British people infuriated him. "No sense of order," he would complain. "It'll bloody well do them good to be invaded."

In person Lionel was scrupulously clean and neat. He worked as an audit clerk and was exempt from call up because he had a withered arm, the only thing he shared with Stalin. He went off to work each morning wearing a pin-striped suit, and returned at the same time almost every evening to tell stories of the petty cheating or outright crookedness practised by the business men for whom he worked. Lionel tolerated, and in a way even admired, their villainy, rather as a zoologist may feel some fondness for the wildness of the animals he is hoping to tame. He was concerned and worried, not by the
88

progress of the war but by the poor quality of the revolutionary workers so highly valued by Rex, and also by the divisions in the movement. Lionel and Rex were adherents of the R.S.L., the Revolutionary Socialist League, who were deeply divided from the other English Trotskyist group W.I.L., the Workers International League. W.I.L. had more members than the R.S.L., they had their regular periodical W.I.N. (Workers International News), they obtained what little publicity was given to the Trotskyists in those days. Should the R.S.L. join forces with W.I.L., or were the W.I.L. leaders mere unscrupulous adventurers? This was a subject for endless debate between Lionel, Rex and other members of the group, including our local factory workers Bert and Joe. In the meantime leaflets calling for an end to the war and for workers' control of industry were printed and brought round to the house by furtive-looking boys on bicycles. Did Mr. Strong ever wonder about them, or about the grubbiness of Bert and Joe when they came round to meetings? Strangely enough, there was no indication that he did, or that he was worried by the song that Lionel sometimes untunefully sang:

Send out the Army and the Navy,
Send out the rank and file,
Send out the gallant Territorials,
They'll face the danger with a smile.
Send out the boys of the old brigade
Who made old England's name.
Send out your mother, your sister or your brother—
But for Christ's sake don't send me.

One of the things that always disturbed Lionel was the way in which members of the group wasted time in idle conversation, drink or sex. He regarded Rex as a figure sinking slowly into a sexual quicksand from which he did not even attempt to escape. "She's *terrible*," he would say half-mockingly and half-seriously when he came home from work and found Rex and Rita in bed, adding, with a precise snap that he sometimes used to finish a conversation: "Oversexed". Rita on her side was concerned about Lionel, whose teeth ground when he was asleep with the effect of a mincing machine powdering up fragments of bone. As we listened in amazement outside his bedroom door—how could his teeth stand the strain?—she would say: "Poor darling Lionel, we all know what his trouble is." Rita was inclined to treat all problems on this level. When the W.I.L. headquarters were raided she was chiefly impressed by the way in which some papers had been discovered on a woman party member. "Hid them in her knickers, silly cow. Of course that's the *first* place the police looked."

My own position in this household was ambiguous. I was a lapsed member of the R.S.L., but still a sympathiser. Occasionally I went to meetings, but I can't recall that I ever did any work in the way of distributing leaflets. I believed like Rex and Lionel that Britain would be defeated by the superior efficiency of German arms and organisation, and regarded a German hegemony over Europe as certain. I believed also, and this belief was not so rare then as it is today, that an inherent virtue rested in the working class, that they were more generous and intelligent than those who had money and property, that only under working-class control could there be a good society. K., who came to stay at Denmark Hill and later married me, often woke up screaming from nightmares caused by her fear that I might be sent to a concentration camp, and since I am half Jewish the fear had nothing fantastic about it, but I can't say that I ever felt this, any more than I was frightened by air raids. What did concern me was the question: what should I do when called up? I made up my mind to object, on the ground that the war was being fought for capitalism. I quote from an article, a period piece, written in the summer of 1940:

Both Allies and Nazis are waging war for reasons equally wrong, equally vicious. . . . Indeed, I think organized persecution preferable to the indiscriminate bombing and machine-gunning of troops and civilians.

I wasn't opposed to all wars, only to this one. A ridiculous attitude? "I don't defend my conduct, I explain it." Or less than that, perhaps: I simply record it. My decision was strongly disapproved by Rex and Lionel. Roy, now called up and doing naval training, wrote to me with a touch of irony: "I hope you do it. We must have someone to keep the home fires burning, and to take care of our books."

The illusions of the phoney war, the dreams of that halcyon summer, were shattered by the sound of bombs —so people say. Personally I don't recall that as being at all true. The bombs fell. One of them, unexploded, dropped in the garden at Denmark Hill, making the house uninhabitable. We left Mr. Strong and took a house in Streatham. The bombs fell and changed the face of London. Lionel became a fire watcher, a task which he carried out with quivering reluctance. Rex received his call-up notice. Leaflets were still produced, and disseminated from Streatham, attacking with impartial fury the war, the Communist Party and W.I.L. The bombs fell, newspapers became smaller, there was less food.

A wretched time, people say. I recall it as one of the happiest periods of my life. I have always desired a society in which everything should be impermanent and in which the possession of property and the inheritance of money should be eliminated. It did not disturb me at all to know that the place in which I lived might any day be destroyed, and the routines by which most of us live become meaningless. I know now that I shall never see such a Utopia, but life in London at this time gave a hint of it, as life in Russia must have done in the months after the Revolution. For such a temperament London in those days was in many ways an ideal city. The journey to work was an adventure and an absurdity —twice a bomb fell within a hundred yards of the bus in which I was travelling. Living became a matter of the next meal, the next drink. The way in which people behaved to each other relaxed strangely. Barriers of class and circumstance disappeared, so that London was more nearly an equalitarian city than it has ever been in the last quarter of a century. Was it mere romanticism that discovered "new styles of architecture, a change of heart" in the bombed places? For a few months we lived in the possibility of a different kind of history. It only just needs saying that the successive pieces of "bad news" which distressed many people, expressing the consolidation of Nazi power throughout Europe, were to me only an expected proof of an old order breaking up, a new one of perpetual repression and revolt taking its place. The sense of two "real" worlds, openly repressive and equalitarian, struggling with each other, was exhilarating. This division of society into opposing forces seemed to me as real as the peace of 1945, when it came, was to appear an illusion.

During these months Rex went into the navy, where he was able to preserve his beard. Both he and Lionel were enthusiastic about the chances for propaganda that would be open to him. Lionel started to grow vegetables by hydroponics, in anticipation of a coming food shortage. At this time also it turned out that Lionel's attitude towards women, whom he treated as slightly ridiculous but endearing kittens, was by no means devoid of attraction. Girls outwardly as respectable as himself, clerks and secretaries, would come to the house in the evening, take down the details of some virulent memorandum, and then stay the night. "Of course they all want the same thing," Lionel would say with gloomy resignation afterwards. "It wears you out. But she may be useful, she's got a typewriter. I've asked her to bring it along tomorrow." Rita observed these developments with delight mingled with some mortification. Who would have guessed that sexless Lionel was like that? She was unhappy after Rex's departure and went about the house miserably singing:

When there isn't a man about you do feel lonely,
On your only,
Really and truly on the shelf,
Nothing to do but play with yourself,
When there isn't a man about.

But Rita could never be unhappy for long. We gave a party and she recovered her spirits.

Only two things marred my own pleasure in this invasion year (for people thought of an invasion as likely long after the possibility of it had disappeared), the sudden switch of Soviet policy after June 1941, and the problems of my tribunal. The Trotskyist attitude towards Stalin's Russia was contradictory. On the one hand it was condemned as corrupt and bureaucratic, on the other sentimental hopes that Stalin had not forgotten his revolutionary past remained. These were continually being disappointed and Roy, who was by no means sympathetic to R.S.L. or W.I.L., wrote to me from a training course in Aberdeen: 'I'm afraid Lionel is mostly right: Stalin is really Ramsay MacDonald with a dyed moustache. Bill (the Communist propagandist William Rust) was here on Sunday with a platform of respectable town councillors. My reports are that he said support Churchill, but said it with a Left accent. It is too much for us parlour revolutionaries." This disturbed me more than my inevitable rejection by the Tribunal, a rejection inevitable because the idea of objecting on political, as distinct from religious or pacifist, grounds had no chance at all of success. I can't recollect in any detail what happened at the hearing and the subsequent appeal, and retain only

94

the remembrance of three oldish gentlemen sitting in a small room, and muttering to each other with no particular air of friendliness to me. Rex spoke at my first hearing, but I canot think that his high excitable voice carried any more conviction than mine. Roy sent a letter of support—very sensibly he had looked at the National Service (Armed Forces) Act to see what was required, and had "found that *morality* was the key word, so I plugged that". This, in combination with my own obscure grounds of objection, must have provided an air of comic confusion which was compounded by the letter written by my brother A. J., which began magisterially "Gentlemen of the Tribunal", and stressed that I was simply too nervous to fight:

> He has from childhood been subject to various forms of physical squeamishness. To this day, for instance, he cannot travel in a motor vehicle for more than a few miles without being physically sick; and he has an excessive nervous reaction to wasps, bees, and other more harmless winged insects. . . . Apart from the disabilities mentioned above, his sight is so myopic that there are few military duties that he could perform with safety to himself or to others. . . .

This eloquent but hardly convincing plea did not move the Tribunal. At the appeal I brought up a fresh battery of witnesses including George Woodcock, the Anarchist editor of *Now*. I am not sure whether I followed Roy's advice: "You must lose your aestheticism and recover your morality; less Henry and more Ruskin," but if I did the result was the same.

It is difficult to see all this now as anything but comic, and I think I felt this at the time. I suppose one could say that the whole process, which went on for several months, showed the tolerance of British democracy in treating even such an unworthy objection as mine, but I could never see officialdom of this kind except as something stupidly mechanical which should be cheated if possible. Still, my rejection posed a problem. Should I go to prison or allow myself to be conscripted? The question was solved for me in a manner appropriately irrelevant to moral considerations when K. and I got married. A soldier's wife would receive an allowance, the wife of a rejected objector would get none. Obviously it would be better to accept the call up, since the money would be very handy. I would readily agree with anybody who said this proved that there was nothing conscientious about my objection.

K. and I went off from our wedding luncheon with Rita, to spend three days of honeymoon at Poole in Dorset, where Rex was stationed. He had been assigned to one of the small boats that patrolled the Channel, and seemed immensely well and cheerful. When I asked him how propaganda work was going he smiled, stroked his beard, and was evasive. It turned out that he never talked about politics, nor apparently thought much about them now. "They're a pretty good bunch of chaps," he said, dropping into out of date slang, and when I suggested that his tacit support of the war was hardly a proper attitude he shook his head. "I don't know about that, Julian. I don't know much about anything any more." When this was reported back to Lionel he shook his head sadly but without surprise. He considered back-sliding to be the natural condition of unregenerate mankind.

In the meantime a reprieve came to me, as it often comes to those who accept their fate. I was offered a job in the Birmingham factory of Midland Paint Sprayers, which would give me exemption from Army call up. I was to work as a progress chaser, and I took the job without hesitation. It would be much better paid than the Army, I had (I hope I have made clear) no patriotic scruples, and I had after all been chasing progress most of my life. Birmingham seemed a dull city, but the chase for progress was rather agreeable. The factory was making spraying equipment used mainly for camouflage work and I produced prettily coloured charts, less common then than they are now, showing the movement of each item through the works, and explained this to foremen who were astonished equally by my manner and my beard. "He's just like a bloody professor," one of them said wonderingly in my hearing. I was separated from K. who, also in pursuit of a reserved occupation, had taken a job in London with the B.B.C. Removed from the basilisk gaze of Lionel I spent most of my evenings reading Shakespeare, Trollope and Henry James. What was Henry's secret? Roy and I exchanged letters about it. "He drank little, smoked less, fucked not at all—there aren't many more things that could counterpoise that immense façade of the complete literary figure," Roy wrote. "I think he was really a woman, like George Eliot." Pursuing indirectly this thesis I wrote an essay about *What Maisie Knew*.

D

This agreeable interregnum was ended after a few weeks by a letter and a telephone call. The letter contained my call-up notice. I took it to Jenkins, now the firm's managing director. He was reassuring. The whole thing must be a mistake. Was progress chasing not essential work, was my occupation not after all magically reserved? "You're certainly essential to us here," he said as he reached for the telephone, but when he added that although I must report they would soon have me out, and that they would make the strongest possible protest, I knew my cause was lost.

The telephone call came a couple of nights later, from K. It was to tell me that Rex had been killed. His boat had been on a routine patrol when a German plane machine-gunned it. Nobody else had been hurt. It was an absurd enough end to a trivial enough life, yet for me these two things had a linked significance without any logical basis. I have often wondered since then if I should, after all, have gone to prison, whether this would in some way have justified an objection in which I did not believe and have been an assertion of faith in the future. When I put down the telephone, and a few days later reported for duty at an Army unit, I was turning my back as Rex had done on the world that for us represented reality, acknowledging that the war we had never fought in was lost, and that what we had thought of as our human possibilities would remain for ever unfulfilled.

You're in the Army Now

April 30, 1942. I shaved off my beard, a necessary preparation before joining the 57th Tank Regiment, R.A.C., at Warminster, Wilts. A strangely innocent melancholy egg looked out of the glass, yellowish but pale. Eighteen years passed before I resumed the beard, and then perhaps it was a mistake. The first beard was black, glossy, springy, alert, the second dry, wiry and dismayingly patched with white. My first beard was a provocation, the second merely a concealment.

★

Perhaps it is true that early manhood is the time of greatest anguish, but it is also the time of greatest resilience. With so much of life to lose we readily accept the idea of losing it, and the violent changes imposed by war, death, revolution, appear a matter of course. In middle age almost every change seems intolerable,

D*   99 each obituary notice of a friend clangs like a warning bell. "It is not by our beliefs that we live but by our habits": one might change that epigram of Radiguet's to something less cynical and less witty, but sadder. In youth our beliefs make life possible. Later only our habits make it endurable.

In the train to Warminster I had for a short time that feeling of making an enforced clean break with the whole of my past that is in a way euphoric. Goodbye, unconscientious objections, I said to myself, you're in the Army now. This sense of being truly a part of society, one among all sorts and conditions of men, which the intellectual simultaneously longs for and fears, buoyed me up until we changed and I saw my companions on the platform. They looked a depressing lot. One carried, like a tattered flag, the *New Statesman*. Boldly, like an old-fashioned spy producing the matching half of his recognitory coin, I drew out the Trotskyist *Socialist Appeal* ("For a Socialist appeal to the workers of all countries"), and we talked. Grimsdell was a big, fair, slow-spoken man who had worked in the advertising department of a firm of baby food manufacturers. He had left behind not merely a wife like me, but also children, and he did not share my view of army life as a new aspect of experience offering infinite promise and menace. He saw it simply as another job, in which it was natural to try to do as well as possible. He handed back my *Socialist Appeal* with a look of some distaste.

At Warminster a sergeant waited for us. "Cheer up, my lads, you're in the Army now," he cried, and we gave an appreciative murmur of amusement. We mar-
100

ched to the barracks raggedly but in rather good spirits, infected by his jollity. That night he came into our room and gave us a general chat about what life was going to be like. "I'm Sarnt Gardner and you're 181 Squad. I'm going to have you for six weeks until you pass out, and I like my lot to be the best passing out squad. You're here to work, I'm here to see you do. Any help you want, you come to me. You work and I'll love you. If you don't work I'm a bastard."

What can one say that is fresh about this kind of Army routine, square bashing, rifle drill, route marches? It has all been said by Julian Maclaren-Ross in that admirable collection of stories, *The Stuff to give the Troops*, which I hope somebody will republish one day. Perhaps Maclaren-Ross and other writers haven't emphasised as much as they might have done the resemblances between the Army and a boarding school, or any other closed institution, the deliberate mechanisation of life expressed in the queues for food and the sign in the dining hall: "If You Take It Eat It", the proliferation of incomprehensible orders, the rules made known only after they have been transgressed, the artificial rivalry that was encouraged between 180 and 181 Squads. And the semi-illiteracy of most of the men in 181 Squad surprised me. All of them could read, but not more than half of them did, and most of the readers confined themselves to weeklies like *Tit Bits* or *Blighty*. Among our forty squad members I should not think more than a dozen had ever read a book.

Personalities soon emerged, the most prominent of them being Trooper Barnacle, a lithe young Cockney who was sharp as a razor on the parade ground. "Bags of swank, come on now, give it bags of swank," Sergeant Gardner would cry, and Barnacle marched with a fine swagger. His arm shot forward at precisely the right height when marching, his rifle drill was impeccably precise. On route marches Barnacle would sing:

> Ask old Brown to tea
> With all his family.
> If he don't come we'll tickle his bum
> With a stick of celery.

Head up, arms swinging, he delighted the heart of Sergeant Gardner. Grimsdell tried desperately hard without great success, and so did his friend Queen, a thin nervous former insurance agent who like Grimsdell was determined to become an officer. My euphoria had vanished within hours, and I was one of the worst men in the squad.

This was soon remarked by Barnacle, and he quickly recognised another fact. "Hey, Jewboy," he shouted one day. "Sling us the *Mirror*, will you." The words brought me up with a shock. A conscientious atheist and pork-eater, I rarely think of myself in any way that concerns religion or nationality, and it was disturbing to discover that for perhaps half the squad I was obviously a Jew, and to be distrusted on that ground alone.

Barnacle called a Jew a Jewboy as he would have called a Negro Sambo. In a sense he meant nothing by it, or nothing beyond an automatic expression of certain beliefs. I suppose the chief of these were that a Jew was a foreigner and inferior to an Englishman (my inadequacy on the parade ground bore this out), and that he would always try to obtain by Semitic craft what he could never get by merit. Many of his remarks to me were coloured by this feeling. "Bloody rotten fat beef today," he would say. "But I notice you got a nice brown outside bit. Slipped old Fanny a couple of bob, eh? Trust the old chosen race." Under this mild tormenting I adopted that dismal mask of *the persecuted* that fits so easily on Jewish features. It seemed to me that Grimsdell and Queen, who had been very friendly with me in the first couple of weeks, were no longer anxious for my company. I attributed this to their dislike of Jews rather than to what was no doubt the real reason, a feeling that association with a member of the awkward squad, and a subversive one at that, might prejudice their later O.C.T.U. chances. My only associate was another reject, a pale rat-like scuttling creature named Frewin, who would say in the mornings: "Why should I get up when I've got the health and strength to stay in bed?" With Frewin, whose object was to evade every possible duty, I spent hours in the Naafi, drinking beer, eating cheese puffs, listening to popular songs on the radio:

> I never said thanks
> For that lovely weekend,
> Those few days of heaven
> You helped me to spend.
> The ride in the taxi
> When midnight was flown,
> And breakfast next morning
> Just we two alone.

Taxis, shared breakfasts, leisurely instead of hurried and unsatisfactory sex, that whole world of freedom or its illusion, the sentimental song brought it overwhelmingly back. In the many *Us* and *Them* divisions that exist during a war, that between civilians and those in uniform is among the greatest. We were not allowed to go home in this basic training period, but my wife K. spent a weekend in Warminster, sleeping in the bathroom of the Bell Hotel. Her prettiness was a matter of surprise and envy to other members of the squad, including Barnacle. "Nice piece of crackling, your wife," he said. "Lucky old Sym." With the true feebleness of the persecuted I was warmed by his praise. When she returned to London I felt as if I had been left in prison.

My position in the squad reached its nadir on the night before we were due to pass out. Sergeant Gardner came into the barrack room and had a chat with everybody, rather in the spirit of a football manager giving encouragement to his team. To Frewin and to me he said simply that we should not be needed on the passing out parade. The Sergeant had by now inculcated a strong corporate spirit into 181 Squad. They were determined to be the best ever handled by Sergeant Gardner, and the relegation of two squad members to the barrack room was simultaneously desired and deplored. "You know why you're not bleedin' going on the parade, don't you?" said Barnacle, who had recently been made an acting unpaid Lance Corporal. "You'd let the squad down, that's why." On the following day Frewin and I watched through the window the group on the square marching, wheeling, presenting arms, under the eyes of the

PR
6037
Y57525

Symons, Julian, 1912–
    Notes from another country. London, London Magazine
Editions, 1972.

    147 p. 20 cm. £1.80

I. Title.

PR6037.Y5Z5   828'.91209 [B]   72–171192
ISBN 0-900626-76-3

Library of Congress   73 [4]   MARC

B 72–19063

Colonel and his squadron commanders. Then the Colonel moved slowly along the ranks accompanied by Sergeant Gardner, both as straight as telephone poles. Occasionally the Colonel stopped and dropped a word—of commendation or disapproval? It was impossible to tell, but neither 180 nor 181 Squads was judged to have given the best display. Later that day the list of allocations for further specialist training as drivers, mechanics, gunners, was put up. Grimsdell was to be a gunner, Queen a driver. In the whole squad only Frewin and I remained unallocated. We were put on fatigues, which meant cleaning latrines, tidying paths, weeding the Colonel's garden.

This relegation to a category of uselessness introduced me to a sodality of similar rejects. Nobody was much interested in us, and although we were given assignments it was rarely necessary to carry them out. Told to clean the latrines we would spend ten minutes there and then slope off to the Naafi, from which a sergeant or corporal would occasionally clear us out. Among these rejects was the painter Carel Weight, a sad figure who took his duties more seriously than I, and was rarely to be seen in the Naafi, perhaps because he could not bear the treacle of popular songs that tasted like nectar to me.

> Tell me I may always dance
> The anniversary waltz with you.
> Tell me we shall always make
> Our anniversary dreams come true.

One day I was summoned to see the Adjutant. Jenkins

at Midland Paint Sprayers had seemed confident that they would get me out, and side by side with the desire to be cut off from the past there went, as I have already mentioned, the longing for a return to it, a lollipop just out of reach. Sure enough, as I saluted and said "7956780 Trooper Symons J." I glimpsed on the desk a letter on Midland's writing paper, and the Adjutant, a brisk Major, began by saying that my employers appeared to think that my services were essential to them. Was the lollipop to be put into my hand, were my anniversary dreams coming true? His next words destroyed that hope. "They've been told that there is no question of your release. You're more essential to us. I just wanted to let you know the position." He went on to tell me that I had been made a clerk and that I was to report to B Squadron office for training.

The verdict did not greatly depress me. I have always preferred knowledge to uncertainty, and although I received further letters from Midland telling me that they had not given up, I put the thought of release out of mind. The sentence was final, and like all such sentences seemed to be for life. My fate was decided, I was to be a clerk. The fact was put up that day on orders and I felt a small, wretched glow of pleasure when Barnacle said with ineffable condescension, "Glad to see you're fixed up, good work." I was placed automatically in a different class from Frewin. I had not let the side down completely after all.

Two or three weeks later the regiment moved to Catterick.

*

Life in the Army as I knew it was little concerned with the war. It was of course the reason for our existence, yet it remained an abstract concept. Men were being trained for *the war*, when trained they were sent away, but all this was theoretical. We saw no dead, no wounded except those occasionally injured on manoeuvres, suffered no air raids. I had been much closer to such realities of war when the bombs fell round me a few months earlier in Streatham. Other realities we did encounter: the boredom, confinement, obedience to orders, which is what army life means when it does not mean terror and anguish.

To my astonishment I found that my position as a Squadron clerk was an envied and in some ways enviable one. Clerks might be the arseholes of the Army in the eyes of a gunner or driver mechanic, but to Company Commanders eager for a quiet life they were infinitely more valuable than the men who were being trained. Typewriters were as rare in Army offices as they are now in police stations, and when I said that I owned one, the week-end pass that had been impossible to obtain was given to me immediately so that I could go to London and bring it back. In the division between Ins and Outs, Us and Them, I had moved with no volition of my own to the other side, at least within the Army. I was at the heart of things, I knew who was going on courses and who had been recommended as officer material, I was even able occasionally to get week-end passes signed for other people. Grimsdell and Queen became friendly with me again.

The office was run by a lance corporal named Harold

107

Jackson with the help of various temporary figures who passed through it while being trained as clerks. Jackson was permanent, because a perfectly genuine ear complaint which gave him some pain had caused him to be graded C 1. He had been a local government officer in the Midlands, and was an extremely efficient and painstaking clerk whose efforts were dedicated to living through the war without seeing a shot fired in anger. Major Stone, the Squadron Commander, believed with some justification that his office would be in chaos but for Jackson, the single Squadron clerk allowed by establishment. We soon became extremely friendly, and by a special dispensation were allowed to sleep in the office in a space behind the filing cabinets, an unhygienic arrangement which Harold justified to the Major on the ground that we would be on duty twenty-four hours a day.

Members of 181 Squad would come in and ask questions about their future, questions which Harold, who had seen many squads come and go, regarded impatiently. "You'll know soon enough, just fuck off and enjoy yourself," he would say. "Don't be so fucking anxious to get away from here, it's worse where you're going." Sometimes he would say to me, "You're too soft with 'em, Sym, they're just bleeding nuisances." Recollections of my own previous misery made me gentle with Grimsdell and Queen, who had been recommended for O.C.T.U. and came in almost daily to ask whether their postings had come through. "On the whole, Harold, you're too hard on them", I would say, and would be answered by a brisk fart. "On the hole, Sym, yes, but on which hole?"

Harold was more amiable than I am making him sound, and we soon became absorbed by the problem of saving me from the fate that had befallen all the other temporary clerks, of a speedy overseas posting. Could this be done? Probably not, but at least we could try. Major Stone himself, a gentlemanly near-midget, was sympathetic although unhelpful. "You're a very good chap, Symons, like to keep you," he said. "Understand you're a bit of a writer and that comes in useful. Just isn't possible, though God knows there's enough work for half a dozen people out there." In this illusion lay the best hope of my being kept on, and Harold and I fostered it assiduously. In fact there were busy times, but there were other whole days when I sat at my desk looking out through the three large windows that made up one office wall. To the left new roads were being built, immediately in front were the football pitch and the yellow basketball posts, a little further away stood the officers' mess in red brick and other ranks' huts, long and low. In the distance the trackpins of the tanks glittered as they crawled up to the Yorkshire moors.

These days were spent in a waking dream looking at the life outside which seemed to have passed me by; speculating on my own likely fate; reading *Socialist Appeal* and *Fourth International*, writing about the office and the wall chart I kept (my passion for order had full play, and the chart was much admired by Major Stone and by visitors) for *Partisan Review*:

In front of me, covering a whole wall of the office, is a big board covered with grey cloth. On this grey cloth, held between stretches of white tape, are some hundreds of tickets with the names and numbers of the men in my Squadron. The tickets are variously coloured—pink for new recruits, pure white for potential officers, yellow for the permanent staff, blue for men earmarked for posting to special places, orange for men available for posting anywhere. The board has many subdivisions; one batch of tickets for one squad of men is kept separate from the next batch of tickets by the strips of tape. As the weeks pass tickets are moved across the board from left to right, the colour of the tickets is changed as men become potential officers, potential instructors or merely available for posting. The board shows in a moment the location of any man in the squadron, the men in detention, the men on leave, the men in hospital. To be responsible for it, to move the tickets along and finally tear them up when men are posted away from here, is to feel disturbingly the sensation of power.

I went on to stress in the article what I have said already about the remoteness from the war one felt in these barracks, where a man's fate was represented by a ticket on a wall. At A.B.C.A. (Army Bureau of Current Affairs) lectures any attempt at general discussion about the nature of Fascism or any similarly touchy subject was cut off very quickly. We were not there to talk about such things, but to be told about the progress of the Eighth Army's campaign in Italy or about the resources of Latin America. The wall newspaper which I ran at this time was stopped when I made an attempt to discuss general issues. "*The war* is not taboo but it is neglected: something much less important than the Sergeant Major's voice."

Company Sergeant Major Nutto was probably the most important figure in the Squadron, and also, in my life at this time. Thick and square, with a broad flattish sneeringly handsome face, he was one of the few soldiers in the camp who had seen active service and who, rarer still, wanted to get back to it. He had suffered a head injury in France just before Dunkirk and suffered from blinding headaches, but he had been downgraded only from A1 to A2, and lived in expectation of the day when he would be posted to a unit going overseas with promotion to R.S.M. C.S.M. Nutto's characteristic manner was one of heavy sarcasm and he did not trouble to conceal his contempt for Major Stone and the junior officers, who were all afraid of him. From the day I arrived in the office Nutto regarded me as a slightly fascinating but annoying curiosity. The mask of the persecuted had vanished under the influence of Harold's friendship and the comfortable office life, but Nutto did his best to bring it back. Standing in the centre of the room, thwacking his thigh with his swagger stick, he would say:

"I bet you lived in London, eh, Symons? And I bet they used to think you were a right sod when you were with your Jewboy friends. They got us in this war, you know that, don't you?"

"No, sarnt major."

"They bloody did, I'm telling you. What do you say to that?"

"I don't say anything."

"You fucking would say something if we were up in London, I'll bet you'd be taking the piss out of me up there. But you're not in London, you're in fucking Catterick, and that's where you stay till you get posted. And that won't be long." Thwack thwack. "Any news of my posting, Jackson?"

"Don't you think I'd have told you if there were?"

"You bleeding clerks wouldn't tell your own mother the time."

Such encounters were more upsetting to Nutto than to me. He was one of those intelligent but ignorant men who are aware of their own deficiencies, and he felt an uneasy respect for devices like the wall chart. One day he asked me to explain it to him. "Bloody marvellous," he said, at the end. "You're a smart sod, Symons, you know that. You're wasted in this office, ain't that right, Jackson?"

"He does a better job than you would, sarnt major."

"You're too smart for your own good, you fucking clerks. I'll tell you something, Symons, I'm having you on parade Saturday and you'd better look a bit different from the way you do now. You'd disgrace a squad of pregnant nuns. I'm going in to tell 'im now."

For weeks Nutto had been insisting that only one clerk was needed in the office on Saturday mornings, and that either Jackson or I should attend the weekly parade which was compulsory for all except the sick. For weeks we had ignored him, but now crisis point had been reached. He marched into Major Stone's office, and ten minutes later the Major called us both in and said apologetically that the C.S.M. had insisted that one or other of us must be on the parade. "It had better be you, Symons."

On the following day Nutto came in and stood with legs splayed, thwacking his thigh. "Saturday morning then, I'm looking forward to it. Who's it going to be?" No reply. He spoke louder. "I said, which one of you lovely lilies is it going to be?"

Harold turned round from his typewriter. He had a line in mock-indignation that I could never match. "You've got what you wanted, sarnt major. Now if you don't mind we've got work to do." We both clacked away at our typewriters.

Nutto was hurt and bewildered, like a cat who has been told that the mice do not enjoy being hunted. In a way he really liked us, and felt that we should applaud him for winning our game of wits. He snorted and went out.

Nutto's word was law, and on Thursday night I settled down resignedly to polish my belt and badge, which had not been touched for weeks. But Harold was made of harder metal. On Friday afternoon he retired to his bed, and when Major Stone asked for him I said that he was not well. The Major came into our office, and went behind the filing cabinet to the bunks. Harold was lying on one side with a handkerchief pressed to his ear. He moved to get up, but the Major waved him back.

"Sorry you're seedy, Jackson. What is it?"

"My ear, sir. It's discharging." Harold lay back and after a pause spoke again. "I shall have to report sick in the morning, sir."

"Righty ho." Then the Major realised the implications of Harold's going sick. "Symons is on parade."

"That's right, sir."

The Major stared at him. Later he stood in the office twiddling a button on his jacket. "Symons, you needn't go on parade tomorrow. Jackson's going sick. Must have someone in the office."

Harold went sick and the M.O. gave him some different drops for his ear. We did not see Nutto until late on Saturday afternoon when we were preparing to go into nearby Richmond. He spoke with heavy sarcasm. "'Ow's your ear, Jackson?"

"Not too good, thanks, sarnt major."

I never heard Nutto shout, and now he spoke quietly. "Know what you are, don't you? You're a twisting pair of lying cunts. I ought to put you both on a charge."

"Go on, sarnt major," I said. I gestured at the board. "Who'd keep that if we were in the glasshouse?"

Nutto knew when he was beaten. In a way I think he even admired the way in which brute force had been defeated by tricky intellectualism. "Nothing about my posting? I'll be glad to be shot of this place and get back to some real soldiering."

In the meantime, what of my future? I had outlasted all the other members of 181 Squad. Barnacle had come in to shake me warmly by the hand before he left, and to say with apparently genuine admiration that some people knew how to fix it. Frewin had scuttled away, mysteriously transferred to the Intelligence Corps. Carel Weight's talents had been recognised and after painting nudes in the officers' Mess he had been transferred, I believe to become an official war artist. Queen had got a commission in the Royal Engineers, but Grimsdell was returned to unit as unsuitable. Had the *New Statesman* sealed his fate, had he revealed incapacity for leadership? He was desperately upset, chiefly by the social disgrace of being R.T.U., applied for a special interview with Major Stone and hung gloomily about the camp afterwards, often coming into the office. Harold was wholly unsympathetic to anybody who wanted to become an officer, and asked why he couldn't behave like a sensible man and look for a cushy billet. After a month of waiting Grimsdell was told that he would be commissioned as an officer on a transfer to the Pioneer Corps. This was a terrible comedown, but it was after all a commission. He departed, and I was the last member of my squad in the camp.

I had been preserved from posting only by ingenious fiddling with Form 3005. This was the weekly return of squadron strength sent to H.Q. office, a counterpart of the wall chart, and I should have been shown on it as a clerk available for posting. Instead I was concealed, one week as sick, the next as a potential instructor then as a driver mechanic or a man on leave. The concealment had to be done carefully, because if I was shown as a driver mechanic ready for posting and orders came through for all the driver mechanics, we should have to admit that one of them did not exist. Such hazards had been survived for months, but discovery was inevitable in the end. There were persistent enquiries from H.Q. about a second clerk installed at B Squadron when establishment allowed only one, and eventually Sergeant Stiles paid us a visit. He was a snotty, nose-in-air little man, one of nature's snoopers. He addressed himself to Harold.

"I hear you've got another permanent clerk here besides yourself."

Harold made no verbal reply but took out our copy of the previous week's 3005 and pointed to the line "Clerk" and the number "1", I had been hidden that week as a man on leave.

Stiles pointed at me. "Who are you?"

"Trooper Symons."

"What are you?"

"Clerk."

"He's training", Harold put in.

"Training? I've seen him about the camp for months."

"Not me," I said.

Harold knew that it was time for desperate tactics. He threw down his pen in disgust and stood up.

"You want me to run this bloody office on my own, is that it? Up at H.Q. you've got half a dozen clerks polishing chairs with their arses but if I get a temporary you've got to stick your nose in, is that it?"

The Sergeant recoiled. "Remember who you're talking to."

"I don't give a fuck who I'm talking to." Harold had worked himself up into a characteristic semi-genuine rage. "I'm cheesed off. If we made a muck of things you'd come and complain. But you know bloody well we don't, this is the most efficient office in the regiment. All right then, if I'm going to be left on my own I'm putting in for posting. I'll do it today."

Sergeant Stiles retreated, but not for long. There is a limit to the bluffing that can be done successfully from weakness, and we had reached it. Harold did not want to be posted, and Stiles knew it. I had avoided a posting for nearly a year, and Stiles was not the only person at H.Q. who regarded my continued presence in B Squadron as a scandal. A few days after his visit a memo came down from H.Q. to say that Trooper Symons, J., 7956780, was to be shown available for posting as a clerk. I could do nothing but use the last resort of a malingerer. I went sick.

The malingering was not total. For some months I had had an intermittent pain in the upper part of my left arm. To carry a rifle with it, as I had done in my early days, made it ache almost unbearably. I had in mind the vague idea that I might get some treatment which would involve the chance of snatching a week-end leave before my posting. The chance was slim, because our M.O. was notoriously unsympathetic and had the reputation of being able actually to smell a malingerer before looking at him. However, he prodded at my arm and sent me along to the camp hospital.

I took a volume of Eliot's essays with me and was carrying them when, after the statutory two-hour wait, I was examined by Dr. Naylor. The doctor, plump and urbane, a middle-aged soft-voiced smiling baby, was interested in my reading habits.

"T. S. Eliot. Unusual reading for a trooper."

"I am a poet," I asserted boldly.

"Really? You must show me some of your work. I am an admirer of the 'nineties poets. Yeats now, what do you think of him?"

We talked for some minutes about Yeats and then he deprecatingly mentioned my arm. "We'll just have you in and investigate it, you won't mind that."

E   117

The idea that I had a choice in the matter was flattering. I said that I wouldn't mind. I reported back to Harold and my name was removed from the list of those available for posting. Stiles was hardly able to contain his fury. I had been perfectly fit for a year and now suddenly I was sick. What could this be but some outrageous fiddle? He pointed an accusing finger. "I can tell you this, as soon as you're back you come up again for posting, understand?" I did not bother to reply. I knew that I had earned myself only a day or two of grace.

On the same day C.S.M. Nutto received posting orders, but not overseas, and without promotion to R.S.M. He was transferred to another training regiment in his existing rank. He was deeply cast down, and our relations were by now so friendly that I felt sorry for him. We were invited to the booze up he was having in Richmond before he went, a signal honour.

When I reported to hospital I was surprised to learn that I was staying in for a night, more surprised still to be told that investigation meant a visit to the operating theatre. Dr. Naylor was standing outside the theatre as I was wheeled along on the trolley. I began to say that I hadn't realised what was involved, but he cut me short.

"We'll just have a look", he said in his soft voice. I felt a jab in my arm. He bent over me, smiling. "T. S. Eliot and Ezra Pound were much influenced in their early days by your namesake Arthur Symons."

A fine way to go out, I thought, I'm going out to the music of culture. Then I went out. It was the end of my life as a soldier.

Between the Acts

Waking after an operation is a curious experience. Even the word *waking* is misleading, because there is no feeling that a passage of time has elapsed. There is a moment when you lie comatose upon a trolley, another moment when you are in a hospital bed. Did anything happen between those two moments? Evidently, but you are not aware of it, and in this suspension of time there seems to be the prospect of an existence totally changed. The person on the hospital bed is, for a short time at least, not the one who went in on the trolley. His intellectual capacity is blurred, but as compensation his susceptibilities in relation to the objects immediately surrounding him are greatly sharpened and enlarged, so that these objects have a distinct meaningful reality of their own. This dissociation of the intellect from the senses is something that is often felt by mystics, but that I have known only after an operation, and sometimes while drunk or when making love. I suppose the sensation is similar to the experience of those who go on a drug-assisted trip, although the L.S.D. trippers imagine themselves transported into a different world, while I have always been aware that I am in the "real" one, but in a real world where colours, sounds, objects are apprehended with ecstatic or agonising clarity.

The sensations fade within a short time, and I have never been able to express them clearly in words. They lasted longer than usual on this occasion, while my mind struggled to work out what could possibly have happened to me. I had come to hospital so that a trivial ache in my left arm might be investigated, to use Dr. Naylor's equivocal word, and there seemed no reason at all why I should be lying dazed in a hospital bed. Nurses smiled down at me and told me not to move the arm which was swathed in bandages, patients moved about the ward, the sounds to which I had been almost intolerably sensitive grew less intense and became distinguishable as tapping of feet on the floor, wheels of a trolley moving, susurration of voices. At the same time all this seemed part of a new post-operation world, to which the problems of Trooper Symons, J., 7956780, and his hopes of avoiding a foreign posting bore very little relation. I drifted into a state of semi-consciousness, or perhaps fell asleep.

When I next became aware of what was happening, sensibility had retreated and intellect was on the prowl again. I watched eagerly as Dr. Naylor moved with plump urbanity down the ward, pausing only for a moment beside most of the beds. With me, however, he was ready for conversation. In his soft voice, smiling slightly, he told me what had happened.

"When we opened up your arm we found a fibroma, that is a fibrous tumour. It has been removed. Happily, it was not malignant but benign." What tumour would have dare to be malignant when Dr. Naylor's own presence was so manifestly benign? I asked how long I was likely to be in hospital. A week perhaps?

"Longer than that. Quite a while longer. You will have leisure to write poetry, I shall look forward to reading some of your work." Smiling roundly as a full moon he explained that in order to remove the fibroma it had been necessary to sever the radial nerve of the arm. Four inches of nerve had gone, and this radial nerve lesion would leave me with a dropped wrist. He patted one plump hand with another. "We shall give you remedial exercises and it is possible that the nerve ends may grow together again." And if not? "Then I shall perform another operation, a tendon transplant. It may interest you."

He delicately sketched on a bit of paper to show me just what was involved in transplanting the tendons to make the wrist work more or less normally. As he was leaving he said with a deprecating look, "I'm afraid, though, that you must be prepared for a certain amount of permanent damage to that arm."

Permanent damage: the words meant almost nothing to me at the time. I saw only the days immediately ahead, those days extending quite a while longer than a week, a time free from the Squadron Major's amiable ignorant prattle, the Sergeant Major's commands, the tedium of typing movement orders, the whole dismal routine of an Army office. If my existence was not to be blessed by that total change which I had fuzzily envisaged in the first hours after waking I should certainly have leisure to read what I liked, to write when I pleased, to think about possible futures for myself in the world after the war. My arm hung in a sling, the left hand a drooping alien appendage interesting in its very uselessness. It seemed to me that an idyllic period lay ahead.

This impression persisted through the next days when old friends from B Squadron visited me to offer condolences which were also congratulations. "Some say lucky old Sym, I say you cunning bastard," said Harold. He told me of the fury shown by snotty little Sergeant Stiles about my escape from an overseas draft. A temporary escape, of course, but perhaps the hand might be sufficiently dud to keep me in England, who knew? I shook my head and said that such miracles didn't happen. "Give it three weeks and I'll be back."

I wrote an account of the operation for my sister-in-law, whose father was a surgeon, a Major-General in the R.A.M.C., and settled down to try to write. But I had reckoned without my mates. They cried out, groaned, spat, talked interminably to me and to each other, had the radio on from the moment they were woken in the morning until lights out. Several of them were semi-literate and they asked me for help in composing the letters they wrote to wives and girl friends, letters often as naïve and touching as the words they wrote on the back, ITALY and HOLLAND to say I Trust And Love You or Hope Our Love Lasts And Never Dies. The hospital authorities made me adviser to the men on what books they might like among the Westerns and crime stories that came the rounds. I played chess, read a good deal, had literary chats with Dr. Naylor, but wrote nothing. It seemed that I was allowing time to pass during an interval between one important event and the next. But perhaps for some of us the expected climactic events never take place, perhaps life itself is nothing but a long wait between the acts? This thought did not occur to me at the time.

What did become apparent, as the days passed and the thing at the end of my wrist stayed limp and useless, was that I should not be returned to my unit in the early future. Already indeed the life of Catterick Camp, the nightly hands of cards, the week-end booze-ups, the occasional excursions into the bushes with a willing A.T.S. on the way from Richmond back to Catterick, seemed relics of a past existence hardly to be associated with the far from roistering creature who pottered about the ward and had his strength built up (I had lost a good deal of blood during the operation) by daily bottles of beer. After three weeks Dr. Naylor decided to send me to an Army convalescent home a few miles away. He professed to be disturbed by my failure to produce the poems of which he was, it might be said, the patron. At Vauxton there would be peace and quiet. No doubt, as he said, my Muse would flourish there.

A couple of days before I went, however, our friendship ended. He stopped before my bed and, his rubbery features fixed into an expression as near severity as they could assume, said that he wished I had told him of my relationship to the Major-General. It would have made no difference but still, he said with a shake of the head at once reproachful and unhappy, he wished that I had mentioned it. A letter from K. told me the reason for his perturbation. The Major-General's view was that the fibroma was not serious, that the operation was certain to cause permanent damage, that it was totally unnecessary and had been performed only because it gave a chance of undertaking later on the interesting tendon transplant. He had already blasted Dr. Naylor with a letter, and was later to upbraid him in person for using a soldier as a guinea-pig. I saw Naylor quite often after this, when he paid visits to Vauxton, but he greeted me curtly and gave my arm the briefest possible inspection. I felt uneasily responsible for the change in our relationship.

Vauxton was a large country house set in several acres of grounds, ruled over by Dr. Halliday, a savage Irishman whose attitude to the patients was based upon the belief that they were all malingerers. He strode each morning down the line of men, some with useless arms like mine, others with dubious legs, one or two with plaster casts round their broken necks, but all of them perfectly fit apart from these, as he felt, trifling disabilities. It made Halliday permanently angry to see such a set of scrimshankers. Lifting and waggling my floppy hand, glaring at me through heavy glasses, he would say: "Are you perfectly sure you've got no sensation there? Come on now, man, lift the wrist, you're not trying, you can lift it if you want." My condition was similar to that known as Saturday night paralysis, suffered by those who fall asleep when drunk with one arm hanging over the side of a chair. But Saturday night paralysis is temporary whereas my condition was permanent, for I had learned by this time that the chance of my nerve ends growing together was infinitesimal. A true malingerer in spirit, I was in fact unable to lift the drooping wrist even by a fraction of an inch. Halliday's daily inspection was supplemented by the weekly visits of Dr. Naylor, who made no derogatory comment as he lifted my wrist and let it drop, but only looked at me with large wounded eyes.

The thirty men at Vauxton were all recovering from or waiting for operations, and apart from Halliday's inspections and the mild chore of cleaning our dormitories, we were left in complete idleness, temporary drop-outs from Army life. I had Gibbon sent to me and, reading the *Decline and Fall* for the first time, floated gently on the rolling waves of his prose, but a great deal of our time was spent in playing solo or Monopoly, a game which caused even more bitterness in our narrow circle than it does in ordinary life. There was one corporal with a plaster collar round his broken neck who became particularly indignant when his offers for Leicester Square or Bond Street were refused. "You won't let me into the bloody game," he would cry. "You won't give me a chance; all right then, I'm finished. I've done with you lot." Throwing in his cards and money he would rise from the table, his head unnaturally erect, tears not far from his eyes, to return on the following day and push his little boot or motor car hopefully round the board.

What else did we do? I suppose there were plenty of opportunities for homosexual activity, but none took place openly although one old soldier pursued a fresh faced youth named Billy with a good deal of verbal insistence. "I'm on the twist, Billy," he would say. "You want to make sure you're not left alone with me, I just fancy a bit of brown, I'll be up you like a shot." At times he would pounce on the boy and wrestle with him, undeterred by Billy's cries that he was a filthy beast, saying, "Come on now, let's have it out, don't be ashamed of it, I bet it's no bigger than a winkle." Did he ever get his bit of brown, did he even seriously want it? I don't think so, for in this endless idleness desire for sexual contact seemed to have drained away like every other emotion. Perhaps, as was constantly rumoured, Halliday put dope into the tea. I spent hours sitting for my portrait to another patient, a Sunday painter whose left arm was in a sling like mine. He would come very close to me, peer at the bumps and sockets of my face and say, "Very interesting. Were you always like that, those little holes in your chin and that mole, have you always had them? And then you've got no cheeks, you know that, don't you." His portrait showed all these features of my appearance faithfully.

I was briefly revived from emotional languor when K. snatched a few days' leave from her job in the B.B.C. and paid me a visit. She stayed at a pub a few miles away, borrowed a bicycle and rode in to see me every day. We were not allowed out of the grounds, and Staff Sergeant Armstrong refused to give me a pass out. However, he relented after spending a boozy evening in K.'s company at the pub. "I've been conversating with your wife, Symons," he said to me afterwards. "I don't want you to get the wrong idea, just conversating, very pleasant." A pause. "Now, you understand there's got to be rules but—you can have a pass out tomorrow since the circumstances are what you might call exceptional." Could I stay the night? This was firmly refused, although I did so without detection.

In retrospect I seem to have stayed at Vauxton for ever, emotionally and physically becalmed, expressing my revulsion from the present by reading Gibbon and Trollope and Jane Austen ("good solid pre-deluge literaature, like mahogany sideboards", as Roy Fuller wrote to me from Africa where he was engaged in a similar course of nineteenth-century novels), reading about the war with the feeling that it was something that happened to other people. But what seemed like for ever was in fact only three months. After that time the doctors gave up hope of my nerve ends joining together and I was transferred to Botleys Park Hospital, near Woking, for my tendon transplant. So Dr. Naylor was deprived after all of his operation, and although in the end I dare say he was glad to be rid of me I felt that I had somehow behaved badly to him. After the second operation I had again, and very vividly, that sense of a new world waiting for me, and under the charge of a nerve specialist improbably named Byron M. Unkauf began to write poems, stories, articles for magazines, to emerge again cautiously into the present.

*

At least, that's the way it feels now. Yet in writing of the past, how one transforms and insensibly idealises it, how above all shape and form are imposed upon something which at the time appears a flux of events in themselves sufficiently meaningful. Looking at the scraps of personal correspondence salvaged from those months I find references to people I can no longer remember, acute concern expressed about uncaught trains, confusion over telephone calls, arguments about the merits of social theories put forward in quickly defunct magazines. In re-creating, perhaps even creating, the past we make it inevitably purer and more intelligible than it ever was as seen in the context of a single experience. What we miss out is the vital trivia, like the question in a letter of Roy's referring to my proficiency at snooker: "Will you, with your dropped wrist, be able to make a bridge for your cue? That seems to me important." And there are many kinds of forgotten trivia. A letter of K.'s reminds me that at this time I was much concerned about the future of a woman friend who was, K. told me, "going to live with that young man we met in the Salisbury. . . . I was aghast at this but she said he was madly in love with her and would be a great comfort, although very *anti-semitic* and not very intelligent. She said she felt happy and settled and though she knew you would not approve was writing to you." No picture is complete, of ourselves or certainly of other people. We always put down a personal or imagined truth, even when with the help of memoirs, letters, interviews, tape recordings, we try to evoke a literal one.

Yet the personal truth has its validity for it is, after all, the only thing that we know. The sense of increasing freedom, of a changing society offering undreamed-of possibilities, that I briefly felt was no doubt connected with the fact borne in upon me with each passing week that I might be discharged from the army. Dutifully I went to have my wrist waggled by the girl my Cockney friend Ginger called the massoose, coated my wasted arm with hot wax, clumsily operated a hand loom, watched with detached interest my fingers take on a degree of flexibility, but there were limits to what could be done by a tendon transplant. Although my wrist was now fixed instead of being dropped, Dr. Naylor had been right in warning me that my arm would never be the same again. There was no reason why I should not have done some clerking job in an Army stores or office, but dark hairy Dr. Unkauf seemed in no doubt that I had been atrociously done by, and had earned my discharge. I always suspected that some ukase of the Major-General's was responsible for my benevolent treatment, although he never expressed any sympathy in words and when we played billiards after the war went no further than to comment on the awkwardness of my bridge.

During these waiting months freedom was not only mental but physical. I went up to London in hospital blues, often without a pass, dodging in and out of station lavatories to avoid the attention of military police. My arm was still in a sling, and I hardly liked to refuse the seats offered by women in trains. One or two bits of literary London opened their arms to me, and I dropped gratefully into them. New magazines appeared or were promised. George Woodcock's *Now*, the most intelligently edited of the wartime magazines, emerged from the shadows.

The new or revived politico-literary magazines were more to my taste than the bohemian caperings of Tambimuttu's (*Poetry London*) or the hedonism of Cyril Connolly's *Horizon*, about which I had written without friendliness. "Why were you so miffed about *Horizon*?" one of its contributors asked me long afterwards. *Miffed*— long afterwards or not it is still a period word, almost one might say with a touch of exaggeration a *Horizon* word, expressive of the magazine's air of keeping a flag flying for a social as well as a cultural élite. I confessed to having been unreasonably miffed, yet this battle of players against gentlemen, puritans against hedonists, Goths against silver-age Romans, is a permanent one in twentieth-century Britain. Certainly a study of *Horizon*, its editorial attitudes and social ambiance, the general preference shown in it for the bland over the abrasive, is essential to an understanding of the literary forties in England. Today the gentlemen are on the defensive, but there are still reasons for being miffed about (to take a small instance) the seriousness with which a book about the talentless Brian Howard, talentless perhaps but amusing and *one of us*, was recently treated. It is a mark of Connolly's tolerance, that tolerance so unwelcome to barbarian Goths, that I was one day asked to tea and invited to write an article. "You look like André Breton," he said, a remark I took to refer to my pyjama-like hospital blues rather than to my features. But the warmth of those early words was rapidly dissipated in the refined air where much may be suggested but little that is outspoken said, an air I have never been able to breathe for long without retreating to the oxygen tent of a football match or a crowded pub. I was not surprised a few months later to be called by the editor a fox without a tail, and to be stigmatised by another contributor as a neurotically jealous and completely destructive writer and critic. Abrasiveness was not wholly unknown to *Horizon* when dealing with Goths.

It was a day in winter when I stepped out of the army. I thought to the last that some trick might be played upon me, that the examining board would express admiration of my one perfectly good arm and say that my dud one was not so bad as all that. Sure enough they looked carefully at my left arm, exclaimed at the flexibility of the fingers, asked me to grip their hands and showed surprise at my strength. I feared the worst, but it proved that they were simply assessing the amount of the pension that I was astonished to receive.

Back to life then, back to civilian sunlight. The nine months' gestation in hospital was over. Surely I must have emerged as somebody different, surely every experience would be new as burnished brass? Such illusions helped to sustain my mental equilibrium. There lay ahead in reality the world of doodle-bugs and V 2s, of dried eggs and points rationing and planned scarcity, the world in which it was asked whether any journey was really necessary, a world of order and limitation rather than of telegrams and anger or even of love and suffering. This rational world in which I have lived ever since is for the most part congenial to me, but I recognise its limitations. For those who discover as rarely as I have done that deeper (is it deeper?) river of meaning where the intellect is submerged in the senses, events must always seem comic even when they are most agonising. This comedy extends a long way past my

131

ridiculous experiences in the Army. If these were absurd, then the experiences of the bomb and the concentration camps were irrational absurdities too. It often seems to me that all rationalists are caught in the terrible mechanical logic of the twentieth century, and live in an illusion of will. The vicious and heroic actors, as well as those who remain passive and are acted upon, move on paths they never meant to tread, and imagine themselves as participants in some ideal drama that never takes place. They too, like me, are caught between the acts.

Another Country

Those who have never known regimentation cannot understand freedom. To be able to walk down a street without fear of the voice telling you to straighten up or smarten up, to eat meals where and when you like, to stay out at night without a pass, these are not trivialities to those who have been deprived of them. Army life was as easy for me as for most people, but all institutions are in their nature restrictive, none encourages freedom of the body or the spirit. I thought then, I think now, that most of these freedoms are mere comforters, like a dummy for a baby: and yet, deprived of them, I had found myself envying anybody who was not in uniform.

Now, in January 1944, I was out of it myself. K. had taken a third-floor Pimlico flat while I was in the Army. Her job in the B.B.C. supported us both while I looked round for a job. I went to see Mr. Budette at V.L.D. but, although he exclaimed with pleasure at sight of me, and

133

took great interest in my damaged left arm ("Can't move your wrist down, Symons, what an extraordinary thing"), he made it clear that he was not in a position to offer me my old job back. By leaving him for Midland Paint Sprayers I had broken the general arrangement that jobs were kept for those who went into the Army, and I had been too short a time at Midland for them to be legally committed to me. I was unconcerned, for I had no intention of going back to either firm. Labour was scarce, and I decided that I would join K. at the B.B.C. I wrote offering my services, which were turned down out of hand. I wrote to the Central Office of Information, with a similar result.

I was astonished by these instant rejections, and it still seems to me surprising that in neither case was I even called for an interview. At the time I took refuge in the belief that my tenuous Trotskyist affiliations were recorded in an official file. It is possible that this may have been so—when I went to Ireland a couple of years later I had to answer a lot of questions about the object of my visit—but I suppose it is more likely that without the influential friend I did not possess, there was little prospect of breaking into those bureaucratic citadels. Should not somebody opposed to the war in any case have felt doubts about working in organisations furthering the war effort? My anarchist friend George Woodcock had recently refused to accept a fee after being persuaded by George Orwell to broadcast on the Indian service, on the ground that the B.B.C. was part of the capitalist war structure. But I believed, like some other Left-wingers at the time, that since any work you did was bound to "further the war effort", the nature of the job didn't matter. It was what you did outside this job that was important. Nothing could be further removed from the Simon Pure idealism and belief in "direct action" of students and the extreme Left today.

Whether my readiness to undertake official propaganda was rooted in convenience or revolutionary cynicism, and whether I should in fact have done any classical burrowing from within, is of abstract interest since no propagandist wanted to employ me. There I was, to my chagrin, out of work. I cannot remember whether I applied for unemployment benefit, or whether we simply lived on K.'s money plus the small pension given me on discharge (which I tried without success to compute for a lump sum), but we were certainly hard up. I was offered the position of secretary to the owner of a fashionable apartment block, but turned it down when I discovered that the job would involve spying on the tenants. I also rejected a job in a Smith's bookshop, and one advertised as "personal secretary" to an M.P., which meant writing articles under his name, and being paid part of the fee if they were accepted for publication. The M.P. said that I should retain my free-lance status, which was certainly true, since he did not propose to pay me any salary.

Help came, with ironic appropriateness since I disliked the paper, from the *New Statesman*. In the small ads columns there appeared an advertisement which read in part: "Advertising. Interesting appointment offered by important and progressive London Agency. Prev. exp. not essential provided candidate has suitable potentialities." I wrote to the box number, and received a reply making an appointment for me to come and see the undersigned, who was H. F. Crowther. The name of the firm was Rumble, Crowther and Nicholas, and their offices were in Arundel Street, off the Strand. Crowther was a vague, amiable, embarrassed man in his forties. We got on well. I was the subject of what I recognised later as one of his sudden powerful bursts of enthusiasm. I had no experience of advertising, none at all? I had never written a line of copy? That was wonderful, he said, it meant a fresh approach, couldn't be better. And a poet, that was a recommendation. There were one or two poets working in advertising agencies, and they were doing very well, they had the spark. At this point he broke off disconcertingly to quote a couple of lines from "MacAndrew's Hymn", and ask if I liked them. My failure even to identify the poem set him back for a moment, but enthusiasm conquered all. I was taken down a passage to meet my immediate boss. A small, square-jawed man, pipe clenched between teeth, greeted me with a cautious smile. His name was Walker, and in my days as a table tennis player I had met him half-a-dozen times in the London League. I was in.

The money was £400 a year, which was more than I had been paid at V.L.D. Rumble, Crowther and Nicholas was a medium-sized agency, and not in fact a particularly progressive one. They flourished in this curious war-time interregnum for advertising when controls operated over the amount of advertising permitted in newspapers and magazines, and over the size of individual advertisements. In the post-war world they survived but grew no bigger, and were eventually taken over by a larger firm. I soon learned that Rumble was a business bureaucrat who took little part in devising campaigns, although he might express cautious approval of a presentation being made to a client, while Crowther was an eccentric, whose contradictory enthusiasms followed fast upon one another, and were quickly forgotten. The creative director of the firm, and the man who set the tone of its work, was John Nicholas, who belonged to the individualistic past of advertising rather than to its technocratic future. Like many advertising men before and since, he had come into the business because other talents failed him. He had been by turn an I.L.P. orator, a film and stage actor, a stage manager and a playwright. He was also a capable artist, who had drawn satirical cartoons in his I.L.P. days, and later produced many vigorous paintings after Van Gogh. One of these would be sent out each year as a giant Christmas card. One or two of his plays were very nearly successful. During my time with the firm he wrote one which did well in the provinces, was warmly received at the Wimbledon Theatre, and then died for lack of a central London theatre able to take it.

Nick was a Welshman, with a leonine head, a splendid speaking voice, and the presence of a Victorian actor manager. His political ideas had changed greatly since his youth, and he had written an unpublished book outlining the future of Britain under an ideal benevolent Nicholasian dictatorship. He had that capacity for self-deception common in many "creative" advertising men, which I disliked, probably because it reminded me of my father. Thus, Nick might spend a morning discussing with passionate energy the merits of a new advertising campaign. Just before lunch he would burst into the copy department, gather up the three copy-writers, and take them to Beguinot's, a modest Soho restaurant which he said offered the best lunch in London. Over the carafe Algerian he would talk flowingly about the way in which J. B. Priestley reached the heart of the ordinary man, the iniquitous restrictions imposed on us by the Labour Government, the mumbling that passed for acting on the London stage ("Even our fat actors, boy, even our fat actors are no good nowadays"), about the speed with which he would shake the dust of advertising off his shoes after the unquestionable success of his next play. The copywriters, restrictionist Leftists to a man, played up to him powerfully, and he talked eloquently about the lack of vision among young men nowadays. After lunch we all went back to work on another advertising campaign.

Nick was a volatile, engaging and talented man, and it is a mark of my own distaste for ebullient self-deception that made me find a little of his company as much as I could manage. The humorous gloom of Weeks in the art department was much more to my taste. Weeks was an elderly man who had been a pupil of Sir Frank Brangwyn, and exhibited every year at the Royal Academy, producing efficient little landscapes and figure drawings without the slightest trace of originality. He was a friend of Nick's, who had brought him into the firm on a part-time basis. Nick spoke of him with faintly patronising respect, but Weeks had no illusions about his own artistic ability. "I'm no good," he would say over his third pint. "I'm competent, but I'm no good. If I could get a picture, just one picture, on show in the Leicester Galleries I should die happy. But I know I never shall."

I often went with Weeks and a couple of other people from the art department on lunch-time pub crawls combined with visits to picture exhibitions. It was a time when the resources of European art first became apparent after the war to a wide British public, and they provided a shock of excitement for us all. Weeks admired the Paul Klee exhibition at the National Gallery, shook his head over Picasso at the Tate, but tried to learn from them both. Abstraction and odd little figures were the things now, were they? He brought into the office tastefully coloured little geometrical paintings, mock-Klees and sub-Miros, shook his bloodhound jowls, looked at me with his gentle mournful gaze, and said, "I'm afraid they're not very good." He was right. He died without seeing one of his pictures in the Leicester Galleries.

This picture of advertising life is misleadingly cheerful. Unlike Frederick Rolfe, who found the Catholic faith comfortable but the faithful intolerable, I liked many of the people I met in advertising but found the practice of it in the end unendurable. There is a basic dishonesty about the creation of advertisements which goes far beyond the simple untruths of ordinary propaganda. Written and radio journalism are damaging for anybody who wishes to write something that springs from his own mind and beliefs, but advertising is much worse.

There are three possible means by which a writer may maintain himself, outside his writing. He can live off somebody else, either as the unacknowledged pensioner of a moneyed woman or as a drone receiving state benefit; he can take a job totally removed from his preoccupations as a writer; or he can enter the field of near-art, becoming an employee of the British Council, the B.B.C. or I.T.V., an advertising or public relations firm. Advertising is the worst possible choice, because it is the one that may give most nearly the belief that a creative talent is being used. Copy may sound witty, intelligent, even poetic: but in the end wit, intelligence poetic feeling have gone to waste, as they are not always wasted in writing a radio programme or a TV play. What has been written for advertising is rubbish, a let's pretend creation that can only be fully successful if its producer is also momentarily deceived. The advertising creative man is a perfect example of Orwell's doublethink in action. There is no greater possible assurance of Hart Crane's poetic seriousness than his resignation from J. Walter Thompson because he found himelf unable to write copy for a paint called "Barrelled Sunlight".

I worked in advertising for three and a half years, which grew steadily more uncomfortable as I rose in position from junior to chief copywriter, and in salary from £400 to £1,000 a year. When I left I sacrificed financial security, which I have never cared about, and also gave up something in the way of income. The decisive step was George Orwell's recommendation of me to take his place as writer of a weekly book column in the *Manchester Evening News*. Orwell no longer needed the money himself, and was determined to do something for me. The editor had never heard my name, but allowed himself to be persuaded into giving me a month's trial. When the month had extended into three I gave up my job in advertising. I had no contract with the paper, and they could have sacked me at any time, although in fact I wrote the column for ten years.

I was paid £10 a week for the article, which at the time was not bad, and I had another minor source of income. During my time out of work, K. found the typescript of a crime story in a drawer, done on the green paper which I then favoured because I believed it to be friendly to the eyes. She read it, said that parts of it were quite funny, and suggested that I should send it to a publisher. The typescript was six years old, and was the result of a projected collaboration with Ruthven Todd. In 1936 Ruthven had had some sort of job at the Surrealist Exhibition. He shared my liking for crime stories and later, when I lived opposite to him in Pimlico, we planned a book which should have the exhibition as a background, and in which friends should be introduced, libelled, and either killed off or appear as particularly nasty suspects. Ruthven overflowed with ideas, most of them bizarrely ingenious, but he never got down to any actual writing. In the end I wrote the whole book myself, and the most recognisable figure in it was a caricature of Ruthven. When it was finished, I did not even show it to him or send it to a publisher, but put it away in the drawer where K. found it.

The Immaterial Murder Case was not as odd as the book

Ruthven might have written, but it was fairly dotty as crime stories go, with discussions of an art movement called Immaterialism (you painted what was not there, not material), one or two poems meant to parody current fashions, and an art critic found murdered inside a sort of Brancusi egg. The hero drifts through the book looking for a new kind of electric razor. In terms of plot it is appallingly bad—I got into such a tangle that at one point I included a four-page chart showing the movements of the characters, which was done as much for my own benefit as for that of readers. Encouraged by K., I sent the manuscript to Victor Gollancz, probably the one publisher prepared to consider such a zany dectective story. It was published in October 1945. At the time I made about £200 from it, and the same amount from a second detective story. Both books now seem to me deplorably slapdash—the first one I can look at with any approach to satisfaction is *The Thirty-first of February*, in which I embalmed my advertising experience. In 1947, when I gave up an office job for good, I was far from realising that I had found a way of making a living.

★

"I expose myself entire: 'tis a body where, at one view the veins, muscles and tendons are apparent, every of them in its proper place; here the effect of a cold; there of the heart beating, very dubiously. I do not write my own acts, but myself and my essence."

I expose myself entire: Montaigne's claim is one I could not make. There are some things in these thirty-five years that I could not bring myself to write about, because the writing would be too painful, and a good deal more that I have left out because it would be in some way embarrassing, to other people or to me. I have written only what I wanted to be known, and this is true even when I appear to the reader most prejudiced, puritanical, absurd. I must have wished these things to be known, or why should I have written them down? And the claim to total exposure does not seem to me true of Montaigne, Rousseau, even Boswell. The "exposure" of Montaigne and Rousseau is an emotional strip-tease conducted with delicate art, and Boswell's apparent spontaneity, his elaborate confession of lechery and foolishness, are designed always for the benefit of the "James Boswell" who existed in his own mind's eye. Montaigne and Rousseau wrote for posterity, Boswell's self-portrait satisfied his deep need to portray a perpetually sinning and repenting Scot. He practised exhibitionism for himself alone, as though his Journal were a mirror, yet we may be sure that there were some postures that he did not show, some occasions when he turned the mirror to the wall. Nobody exposes himself entire.

I do not write my own acts, but myself and my essence: that seems to me a profound expression of what Montaigne managed so marvellously, and what in a stumbling, partly unconscious way I have been trying to do. Montaigne writes about the education of the young, the nature of friendship, the use of experience and our almost constant failure to profit by it. Not often does he attempt explicit autobiography. Yet as the essays slowly expand in subject and deepen in self-knowledge, we learn

143

to know him better than we know any Frenchman, perhaps any man, of his time. And reading again these pieces about Bonzo, my father and Mr. Budette, life in the Army and in advertising, I see that I have created a self-portrait mostly in terms of other people. What I have put down is not in every detail accurate, but it is all true in the sense that it expresses, as often a literal accuracy might not have done, "myself and my essence".

These notes from another country end nearly a quarter of a century ago. The figure they show, the player of games, the petty gambler, the half-hearted dabbler in revolutionary political ideas will appear unrecognisable to those who have known me only in recent years. Certainly he has gone now, as the friends have gone with whom I went to school and played cards or cricket, they have all vanished as completely as the dead airmen celebrated by Richard Eberhart in his memorable, oddly moving lines:

Of Van Wettering I speak, and Averill,
Names on a list whose faces I do not recall
But they are gone to early death who late in school
Distinguished the belt feed lever from the belt holding
        pawl.

Gasworthy and Catchpole, Fred Horwood and Bogey Maule, names on no list but mine, where are you now? I suppose one reason for writing these pieces was at once to celebrate and exorcise the past.

Looking back then, looking back, how much is there of interest to anybody else in these carefully recorded trivialities? Well, I have always found as a reader that there is something interesting about any life when it is set down with an attempt at faithfulness, with fair candour and without too much show. And some value inheres, I think, in the way these notes depict a special kind of intellectual (a label I covet, not deny) in a particular period. Only somebody who grew up in the 'twenties and matured in the 'thirties would have my hang-ups about class and honours, only a 'thirties intellectual would have expressed his objections so inadequately in a political sense. I started writing these sketches with the idea that each should characterise a friend of mine, well or little known, and that the title for the whole would be *Some of the Lost*. Not much remains of that idea, which proved too difficult to handle in relation to living friends, but the original impulse remains. Looking back, remembering the way in which I expected societies to develop in the 'thirties, and the part I foresaw for myself in that development, I can still hardly believe what has happened. How did we, my contemporaries and I, manage to live like that? From day to day, from hand to mouth, from neglect to evasion, from phoney war to false security. How can all that appear acceptable, how can such false security be viewed with a smiling face?

These very questions would be asked only by a man of the 'thirties, and it would be wrong to end with too solemn a declining fall. When these notes appear between covers I shall be sixty, an age I never expected to see, and just at present I seem to have gone some way towards completing the circle that leads old men back to childhood. I have recently moved to Battersea, not far away from Clapham where I began, I walk down the Fulham Road to watch Chelsea at Stamford Bridge as I did fifty years ago. But these marks of second childhood are, I believe and hope, illusory. My ticket for Chelsea is seasonal, not permanent, and I do not expect to stay in Battersea for the rest of my life. There is no particular significance in being sixty (forty is the deadly year separating youthful hope from adult achievement), and it looks as if I shall reach that age with my mind in reasonable working order and my senses not much impaired. Certainly the enjoyment of urban sights and occasions, which mean so much to me, seems to have sharpened rather than decreased with the years. My prime emotion, if I knew that I was to die tomorrow, would be that "violent resentment" felt by George Orwell when shot through the throat in Spain, "at having to leave this world which, when all is said and done, suits me so well". It suits me too, I should be crying, there is a great deal I still wish to experience and understand, postpone that coronary or street accident for another few years if you please.

For one thing, there is still work to be done on my always cluttered writing desk, notes to be made, a book to organise and then to write. The writing is not what I hoped it would be when I was young, and it is not done in the world I wished or expected to live in, but for the most part it absorbs my attention, and from some of it (especially the organisation of a book, its shaping and fitting to a proper plan) I get great pleasure. This is true, even though the final end, a fragment of social history or a good crime story, is modest. One must learn to use

146

what talent one has, and not try too hard or too often to reach beyond it. Upon the whole I adhere to Montaigne: "I find nothing so lowly and mortal in the life of Alexander as his fancies about becoming an immortal. . . . The finest lives are, in my opinion, those which conform to the common and human model in an orderly way, with no marvels and no extravagances." I have moods in which I do not think this is true: but most of the time I believe it, and then it is a powerful consolation for the fact that I shall never again inhabit the other country about which these notes are written.

M1